DEEPENING
ENGAGEMENT

─────────── ❧ ───────────

*Essential Wisdom for
Listening and Leading
with Purpose,
Meaning and Joy*

DIANE M. MILLIS, PhD
Foreword by Rob Lehman

Walking Together, Finding the Way®

SKYLIGHT PATHS®
PUBLISHING
Woodstock, Vermont

Deepening Engagement:
Essential Wisdom for Listening and Leading with Purpose, Meaning and Joy

2015 Quality Paperback Edition, First Printing
© 2015 by Diane M. Millis
Foreword © 2015 by Rob Lehman

Page 149 constitutes a continuation of this copyright page.

Library of Congress Cataloging-in-Publication Data
Millis, Diane M., 1962–
Deepening engagement : essential wisdom for listening and leading with purpose, meaning and joy / Diane M. Millis, PhD ; foreword by Rob Lehman.
   pages cm
Includes bibliographical references.
ISBN 978-1-59473-584-4 (pbk. : alk. paper) 1. Spiritual life. 2. Spirituality. I. Title.
BL624.M4973 2015
206'.1—dc23

                          2014050112

ISBN 978-1-59473-596-7 (eBook)

10 9 8 7 6 5 4 3 2 1

Manufactured in the United States of America
Cover design: Jenny Buono
Interior design: Tim Holtz
Cover art: © Marina Zakharova/Shutterstock

SkyLight Paths Publishing is creating a place where people of different spiritual traditions come together for challenge and inspiration, a place where we can help each other understand the mystery that lies at the heart of our existence.

SkyLight Paths sees both believers and seekers as a community that increasingly transcends traditional boundaries of religion and denomination—people wanting to learn from each other, *walking together, finding the way.*

SkyLight Paths, "Walking Together, Finding the Way" and colophon are trademarks of LongHill Partners, Inc., registered in the U.S. Patent and Trademark Office.

Walking Together, Finding the Way ®
Published by SkyLight Paths Publishing
A Division of LongHill Partners, Inc.
Sunset Farm Offices, Route 4, P.O. Box 237
Woodstock, VT 05091
Tel: (802) 457-4000   Fax: (802) 457-4004
www.skylightpaths.com

For my parents,
Rosemary and Joseph

The human heart is never completely born. It is being birthed in every experience of your life. Everything that happens to you has the potential to deepen you. It brings to birth within you new territories of the heart.

—John O'Donohue,
Anam Cara: Spiritual Wisdom from the Celtic World

Contents

Part Three   **Cultivating Engaging Communities**

Foreword

Rob Lehman

The more sacred the object of your
search, the nearer it is.
——Soren Kierkegaard

All books are meant to be read, some to be studied,
and a few must be lived. Diane Millis has given us
a book that invites us to deepen our engagement with
daily living, beginning with a way of reading that bridges
the contemplative and active life. Reading her book is
itself a deepening engagement with life. The form is in
complete harmony with its purpose.

We live in a time when the ancient maxim that action
follows being, *actio sequitur esse,* is being recovered as
a guiding principle of relationship to ourselves, others, and the natural world. It is about the integration of
the heart with the head, the inner with the outer life.
Millis's first book, *Conversation——The Sacred Art: Practicing Presence in an Age of Distraction* (SkyLight Paths),

was about sacred conversations. In her new book, she explores the sacredness of all of life.

The Fetzer Institute, the organization I have served and helped lead for the past twenty-five years, believes that the critical challenges of this century, whether the burning issues of violence and war, social injustice, ethnic, racial and religious intolerance, or the ecological crisis—even the survival of life on earth—call for nothing less than a transformation of consciousness. Most of society's efforts to deal with these problems are directed at the surface level, focusing on political and social-economic change. While such approaches with societal policies and programs are necessary, in the future their sufficiency will depend on whether they arise from a deeper awareness, a deepening engagement.

At Fetzer we are exploring how this awareness emerges and can be nurtured through engagement within the communities in which we live and work. We think of our place of work as a relationship-centered community in which each person is *free* to follow his or her spiritual journey in ways that are authentic, and *free* to become a whole person in body-mind-spirit. We refer to such a community as a *community of freedom*. The challenges of integrating the psychological and spiritual dimensions of life into the active life of work are formidable. Yet most of these obstacles arise because we fear going deep enough. Like digging a well, if we don't drill deep we get stopped by the mud and rock and never reach the pure waters of the wellspring.

The relational challenges and gifts of a community of freedom can lead to personal transformation, a shift from a consciousness of separateness to an understanding of one's personal identity as part of an interconnected whole. There is a new freedom that moves beyond the conventional notions of individual free choice to a personal communion, liberating the human capacity for the greatest freedom—the freedom to love.

Is it possible for our institutions of work to become, in the words of American political analyst Yuval Levin, "soul-forming institutions"? If so, what does leadership become? In this book, Dr. Millis clears a path and points the way for those willing to set out on this journey. The personal stories she asks us to ponder and put into practice transform abstract ideas such as "deep engagement" into living realities. Leadership becomes a personal quest and calling. I can well imagine how Dr. Millis's book would provide the basis for organizational formation work, helping all members of a community of work to experience themselves as leaders.

Millis reminds us that such a large vision starts closest to home through the personal relationships in our daily lives. Her guiding precepts, explored in a rhythm of pause, ponder, and practice, provide a beautiful example of how the great ideas and insights of the wisdom traditions manifest in life stories, and how these lessons of life can be the ground from which our own stories grow. The primary focus is not the separate individual but each person participating in authentic, genuine relationships—sacred relationships of love. The place to begin is with our personal relationships with our families, friends, and our colleagues in the workplace.

Introduction

> Don't ask yourself what the world needs.
> Ask yourself what makes you come alive
> and then go do that. Because what the world
> needs is people who have come alive.
> —Howard Thurman, *Violence Unveiled*

As a child growing up in Burkina Faso, François dreamed of becoming president. He wanted to be an agent of change and make a big impact on others' lives. In college, he found himself drawn to the study of sociology, because he loved learning about people. However, after completing a master's degree in sociology the only work he could find in his country was teaching, and he did not feel called to teach. His sister encouraged him to immigrate to the United States. Finding work in the United States proved to be equally difficult, at least initially. He began washing dishes in a restaurant. Over time, the owner of the restaurant entrusted him with more and more responsibility. He soon learned how to prepare desserts and was eventually given funding to attend the French Culinary Institute in

New York City. When asked to describe his life's calling, he sums it up in two words: baker and lover.

I met François in 2013 when I interviewed him for a film series I produce called *Lives Explored*.[1] In this series, we feature stories of deeply engaged persons from all walks of life reflecting upon what gives their lives purpose and meaning. Throughout our conversation, he invoked the wisdom of the sixteenth-century saint, Francis de Sales: *Be who you are and be that well*. As he talked about his current work, I noticed that he didn't focus primarily on his position as a supervisor for Sara Lee Bakery. Rather, his sense of calling at work transcended any particular role in his workplace. He reflected:

> My job is to make sure that the product that we put out there is of higher quality. That's something that is dear to my heart, to put out quality products for customers. At the same time, I want to make sure the people I work with love working with me, enjoy the fact that I interact with them and the fact that I care about them. It's not just about the product; I care about the people I work with, ask them how they're doing, how's their family, the little things that go a long way. The employees like to know that you care about their lives outside of work. I like to be part of their lives, know how they're feeling out of work. It brings a lot of joy to my heart. I come home, and I am happy that we put

> a great product out there and the employees are enjoying working with me and doing a good job and loving what they do. Those are two elements that I really hold dear to my heart.[2]

I have watched François's interview numerous times and featured his story in many presentations. What I cherish so much about his story is his unabashed commitment to offer love and care to those with whom he works. While he fully acknowledges that some people view his love and care as a sign of weakness, he nonetheless persists in engaging others in this manner, as he believes that "you can't fail by being loving to someone. You can never fail in that. It might take time, but there is no way you can fail in being loving."

What Does It Mean to Be Deeply Engaged?

François is one of the leaders I have personally encountered who epitomizes a life of deepening engagement. What most differentiates these deeply engaged leaders from the other leaders with whom I have worked is their overriding concern for their way of being in the world rather than the positions they hold or the roles they occupy. Like François, these deeply engaged leaders consistently speak about their aspirations, including:

- To engage the deepest part of their being—their inner compass, core, or true self.

- To deeply engage others through their curiosity, concern, and generous presence.
- To build communities of deep engagement that cultivate, support, and encourage the practice of love, care, and compassion.

My life has been devoted to working with all those who seek to deepen their engagement with their true selves, engage others more deeply, and build communities of deep engagement. As a spiritual director and retreat facilitator, I meet with individuals and facilitate groups designed to help people learn how to engage with the deepest part of their being. As an educator and college professor, I offer workshops and teach courses designed to increase our capacity to engage deeply those with whom we live and work. As a consultant and coach, I work with leaders in an array of sectors and settings—corporate, education, health care, ministry, nonprofit, and philanthropic—to help them cultivate communities of deep engagement.

In my first book, *Conversation—The Sacred Art: Practicing Presence in an Age of Distraction* (SkyLight Paths), I explored how our everyday conversations offer gateways for cultivating greater self-awareness, awareness of the other, and compassion in our communities. I drew upon insights and practices from many faith traditions that help us initiate more mindful engagement in our everyday encounters. As I travel and teach about the art of conversation, I meet more and more people who are looking for frameworks and language to deepen their engagement in conversations that are often difficult to have in public settings—for example, how to find greater purpose and meaning in the midst of our daily routines, struggles, and challenges. In particular, I receive numerous requests for presentations and workshops on deep listening.

From what I see, there seems to be a growing concern with listening in our current age. As Bob Johansen, former president and CEO of the Institute for the Future and author of *Leaders Make the Future*, observes:

> LISTENING FOR THE FUTURE is hard work. Leaders must learn how to listen through the noise of a VUCA World of Volatility, Uncertainty, Complexity, and Ambiguity. But leaders can make a better future. We need not and should not passively accept any future as a given.[3]

More and more of us are seeking better ways to listen through all the noise as we struggle to make meaning of our lives, especially the many aspects we find most disquieting.

Precepts for Deepening Engagement

Regardless of who we are or what we do for a living, each of us has opportunities to listen, lead, and contribute to shaping a better future. Our capacity to lead does not depend on whether or not we occupy a formal position of leadership. Our capacity to lead a deeply engaged life stems from the qualities—that is, the habits, dispositions, attitudes, and skills—we bring to our everyday relationships and responsibilities.

What are the foundational qualities found among those who lead deeply engaged lives? This is the question I set out to address in this book. In embarking on this quest, I drew on historical and contemporary wisdom figures. Some of them may be widely known, but more often they are deeply engaged people I have encountered in my everyday life. I also draw on my own practices of what I am learning and discovering in my ongoing efforts to engage my true self and others, and to build engaging communities. What you will find in the following pages is not a how-to book, no recommended to-do lists or action steps to follow. Instead, you will find each of these foundational qualities introduced as brief precepts, beginning with a verb. In constructing these guiding precepts, I drew on spiritual teachings from various wisdom traditions. I have articulated these precepts using language, idiom, and images that I hope will resonate with readers of every background—whether you identify yourself as a seeker, a person of faith, a person of no faith, or spiritual but not religious.

Since these are precepts that I continue to practice and experiment with in my own life, I hope that you will do the same. I suspect that you will find some of these precepts appealing, some you may find intriguing, some you may find challenging, some you may resist, and some you may choose to dismiss. Nonetheless, as much as possible, I invite you to try out each of them to discern and discover which ones prove most helpful in deepening your engagement with your true self, others, and the world in which we live.

Pathways to Deepening Engagement

As I began the research for this book, I discovered an address titled "The Sound of the Genuine," given by Howard Thurman to the graduating class at Spelman College in 1980. In it, Thurman (1899–1981), a beloved educator, author, philosopher, theologian, and civil rights leader, implores the audience: "Can you find a way to hear the sound of the genuine in yourself?" He underscores his point as follows:

> The sound of the genuine is flowing through you. Don't be deceived and thrown off by all the noises that are a part even of your dreams [and] your ambitions, that you don't hear the sound of the genuine in you. Because that is the only true guide you will ever have and if you don't have that you don't have a thing. Cultivate the discipline of listening to the sound of the genuine in yourself.[4]

As I read Thurman's speech, I found myself riveted to the image of the sound of the genuine flowing through each of us. From the time I was a little girl, I have felt that there was something genuine flowing through me. Moreover I am especially enamored with Thurman's use of language and word choice. Rather than urging his audience to "listen for the voice of the Spirit," he casts the question broadly, offering his listeners the freedom to discover for themselves what is most genuine in their lives and challenging them to cultivate a discipline for doing so. Yet, he doesn't stop there. He continues:

> So as I live my life then, this is what I am trying to fulfill. It doesn't matter whether I become a doctor, lawyer, housewife. I'm secure because I hear the sound of the genuine in myself and having learned to listen to that, I can become quiet enough, still enough, to hear the sound of the genuine in you.[5]

We don't just listen for the sound of the genuine for the sake of ourselves; we do so for the sake of the other—all others! Thurman acknowledges that we will find ourselves saying: "'Anybody who looks like him or her or anybody who acts as this person or the other acts,' there simply can't be any sound of the genuine there."[6] That is why he beckons us *to wait and listen for the sound of the genuine* in one another. Thurman believes that it is incumbent upon each of us to try to behold and call forth what is most genuine in others, even those who appear disingenuous.

Thurman then describes a third and final movement that stems from our growing capacity to listen for what is most genuine within us and to encourage those with whom we live and work to do the same. He points out:

> If I hear the sound of the genuine in me, and if you hear the sound of the genuine in you, it is possible for me to go down in me and come up in you. So that when I look at myself through your eyes having made that pilgrimage, I see in me what you see in me and the wall that separates and divides will disappear and we will become one because the sound of the genuine makes the same music.[7]

As I read the entirety of his talk, I began to see a developmental framework operative in what he presented in his address to the students that day, consisting of three pathways moving from

- listening for the sound of the genuine in oneself to …
- listening for the sound of the genuine in the other to …
- collectively listening to the sound of the genuine in one another.

Moreover, the pathways Howard Thurman had so aptly described also depicted what I was witnessing in those who lead deeply engaged lives. They are attuned to the sound of the genuine in themselves, call forth the genuine in others, and work to create the conditions in their communities for genuine mutual engagement.

The structure of this book will follow this same developmental trajectory. In part one, we will explore personal precepts for listening within and discerning what gives us passion, purpose, meaning, and joy. In part two, we will consider relational principles and skills for engaging one another in more meaningful conversations. In part three, we will examine habits for cultivating communities of deep engagement.

My hope is that, as a result of reading this book, you will develop or strengthen your capacity to listen within to what is most genuine and most meaningful in your life. I also hope that you will grow in your capacity to lead and deeply engage others in conversations about what is most genuine for them, especially those whose background and life experiences are different from your own. Perhaps the ultimate sign of success of this book will be that more and more of us will have the courage to initiate conversations, within the communities where we live and work, about what most genuinely matters to us. With that, we can begin to act on what matters to us most.

An Invitation: Pause, Ponder, and Practice

Listening through all the noise in our lives to the sound of what is most genuine requires discipline. Disciplines are developed through personal practice and reinforced through communal practice. That is why I have designed this book as a resource for both individuals and small groups. *Deepening Engagement* offers a tool kit for leaders in all sectors and settings. In the following pages, you will be introduced to guiding precepts for you to pause, to ponder, and to practice personally and then discuss with your team in a small group conversation.

Each chapter opens with an inspirational quotation or poem, with which you are invited to pause. This is followed by a reflective essay and evocative questions to ponder. The chapter concludes with a suggested activity to practice in your daily life.

My hope is that all those who read this book on their own will then invite a friend or form a group with whom to pause, ponder, and practice these guiding precepts together.

Pause

The quotations and poems featured in the opening section of each chapter are from wisdom figures in an array of traditions and contexts. Each, in his or her own way, has shaped my understanding of guiding principles for deepening engagement and listening for the sound of the genuine. I introduce you to their wisdom and encourage you to notice whether or not what they have to say resonates with the sound of what is most genuine in your life. To do so, I invite you to:

Begin by removing any unnecessary distractions around you. Close your eyes, and turn your attention to your breathing. Breathe slowly and deeply. Adjust the position of your body so that you are seated in an alert and receptive posture. Sit in a way that enables you to fully receive and fully release the breath from your diaphragm. As you breathe, place your hands on your heart. Notice the vibration and energy emanating from your heart. Notice the energy that moves both *in* your heart and *through* your heart. Continue to breathe at your own pace. As your mind wanders, and it will, gently return to your breath.

Experiment with the amount of time you devote to your breathing. Some days you may have more time to devote to this intentional way of pausing. On other days, you may have as little as a minute. Regardless of the duration, do your best to pause and attend to your breath before reading the opening reflection.

When you are ready, read the opening quotation or poem slowly and deliberately. As you read:

- Savor the words, phrases, and images.
- Notice if there is a particular word, phrase, or image that resounds in the core of your being.
- Name, either internally and/or in writing, the word, phrase, or image that seems to resonate with what is most genuine in you at this moment.
- Continue to savor this word, phrase, or image as you read the remainder of the chapter.

Ponder

In this section, I invite you to ponder with me as I reflect upon this received wisdom. In some cases, I will share the joys and struggles I have experienced as I am learning to apply this principle of deepening engagement in my own life. In other cases, I will feature stories about others' lived experience to exemplify the principle. My hope is that these reflections serve as a catalyst for you to reflect upon your own lived experience. At the close of this section, you will be offered one or more evocative questions to contemplate personally as well as explore in conversation with others.

Practice

The closing section of each chapter presents actions for you to experiment with and test out in your own daily life. In some cases, what I suggest may not seem relevant or helpful in your current circumstances. If so, listen to what is most genuine for you and adapt the practice for the day accordingly. The important thing is to do something each day to connect your intention with action. When it comes to practices, I believe that less is often more. That is why I have designed these practices to be modest and realistic, rather than ambitious and grandiose. It helps to take baby steps as we learn new ways of living and being. Don't let perfection be the enemy of the good. Try to do some aspect of the practice each day as well as you can, given the circumstances you are in, rather than wait for the day when you can do it all well.

The sound of the genuine is flowing through us. Regardless of who we are or what we do, our attention is our most important resource. Let's encourage one another to harness our attention and experiment with ways of listening through the noise that fills our days (and at times may keep us up at night). Together, let's begin to imagine a world where, in the midst of all the vibrations, pings, and ringtones, we consciously listen to the deeper sound, that which is most genuine, within …

   our being,

      the other,

         our team,

            our family,

               our communities,

                  our workplace,

                     and our world.

Part One

Engaging Our True Self

Be Who You Are

Pause

Be who you are and be that well.

—Saint Francis de Sales

Ponder

It was the title *The Great Work of Your Life: A Guide for the Journey to Your True Calling* that initially drew me. In this book, psychotherapist and leading yoga instructor Stephen Cope examines the lives of a number of luminaries and explores how they came to discover their deep purpose. As I read, I was reminded once again that many extraordinary figures lived ordinary lives filled with failure and rejection. Perhaps no more vivid example was the life of Henry David Thoreau, a man who has been referred to as one of America's greatest natural philosophers and, for many, one of the world's greatest writers.

"Be resolutely and faithfully what you are," said Thoreau—not who you think you should be. This guiding maxim captured the essence of a lesson Thoreau learned throughout his lifetime, and particularly during the time he lived in New York City. At the age of twenty-six, Thoreau set off to secure his place in the city's literary scene. After thirteen months there, his efforts to sparkle in the literary salons had resulted in failure. He was not well accepted in this world. Others saw him as "impossibly rough-hewn and ordinary." And, in spite of his efforts to style his prose according to the fashions of the day, his work was widely disregarded and deemed to be mediocre. While there, he only published one short book review.

Cope describes how the pain of this rejection forced Thoreau "to reach even more deeply into his own unique gift. Who am I? What is my voice? What do I have to say? Digging down into his own inner world, and longing for his roots in the woods of Concord, Thoreau—from his tenement in New York—wrote the brilliant sketch on the 'the first sparrow of spring,' which would become one of the most famous passages in *Walden*."[1] Shortly thereafter, Thoreau returned to Concord and began building a cabin in the woods by Walden Pond. As he did, Thoreau increasingly recognized that becoming a writer was less about an outer journey to a specific destination and more about embarking on an inner journey to discover his own voice.

As I read about Thoreau's experience, I was stopped in my tracks. I had to set the book down, attend to what was stirring deep within, and reflect upon what this story was awakening in me. Undoubtedly, it was the following quotation attributed to Thoreau after his return to Concord that captivated my attention more than any other: "I would rather walk to Rutland than to Jerusalem."[2] At a time when traveling to Jerusalem was *the destination* of choice, Thoreau signaled in this single sentence that his focus was no longer concerned with following conventional pathways. He no longer needed to go to places that seemed grand in the eyes of others or avoid those places deemed insignificant by them. The more he paid attention to who he was, the more he realized that traveling to the nearby, seemingly insignificant town of Rutland, Vermont, would suit him just fine.

It takes immense courage to *be who you are*. As pithy and brief as this guiding adage for a life is, living into this way of being is rarely so. It takes time—in some cases a good deal of time—for most of us to grow in our understanding of *who we are*. As Cope observes, "We only know who we are by trying on various versions of ourselves."[3] And, before we can ever hope to *be that well,* it's imperative for each of us to come to terms with *who we are*. Not who we wish we were or who our parents had hoped we would become, but who we are in this moment in whatever place we find ourselves.

To learn how to be who we are and be that well, Cope notes that each of us will undergo an inevitable struggle to be "right-sized." This archetypal struggle is memorably depicted in Thoreau's life. It is the struggle to *find the sweet spot* between the grandiose expectations we hold for our lives and the all-too-real devaluing that occurs when these expectations go unrealized. What often prevents me from taking action in my life is a concern that a given opportunity is not grand enough. I'm tempted to wait for something even better to come along. At other times, I don't make a move because I don't feel smart enough, capable enough, or up to it. And so I keep waiting, oscillating between waiting for the grand opportunity and waiting for myself to improve. Stepping into the sweet spot is an invitation to take the next best step with our eyes wide open, however small it may seem and however ill prepared we may feel. As important as a sense of place might be, no place (be it New York City, Jerusalem, or Rutland) will be the place for us to be who we are until we have discovered a sense of place within us. Once we've done so, it seems that any place we go may be a place of illumination and joy.

✧

> How do you respond to the following:
> I would rather walk to _____
>   than to _____.
> What does this preference reveal to you
> about who you are and what you value?

Practice

This day, do one small activity that you enjoy doing and you do well. It may be going for a run, conversing with a friend, writing a letter, or preparing a favorite recipe.

Make Use of Everything

Pause

Life's work is to wake up, to let the things that enter
into your life wake you up rather than put you to
sleep. The only way to do this is to open, be curious, and develop some sense of sympathy for everything that comes along, to get to know its nature
and let it teach you what it will. It's going to stick
around until you learn your lesson, at any rate. You
can leave your marriage, you can quit your job, you
can only go where people are going to praise you,
you can manipulate your world until you're blue
in the face to try to make it always smooth, but the
same old demons will always come up until finally
you have learned your lesson, the lesson they came
to teach you. Then those same demons will appear
as friendly, warmhearted companions on the path.

—Pema Chödrön, *The Wisdom of No Escape*

Supple like a tree in the wind,
He has no destination in view

And makes use of anything
Life happens to bring his way.
　　　　　—Lao-Tzu, *Tao Te Ching*

Ponder

I remember the night I noticed the shift for the first time. I had just landed back in Minneapolis after meeting with an out-of-town client. As I made my way from the gate to the parking ramp, a tide of travelers disembarking from the airport tram caught my attention. It wasn't their appearance that I noted—as the majority were men dressed in business attire—it was their stance. They didn't look up as they walked, nor did they turn to interact with those next to them. Instead, their gaze remained fixed, at a 45-degree angle, to an electronic appendage in their hands. Momentarily disoriented, I had an eerie recollection of images from sci-fi movies flashing through my mind. At the time, I was witnessing an anomaly. Now, I see these automatons almost everywhere I go. At times, I am one of them.

I continue to have moments like the one I experienced that night at the airport many years ago—moments when I despair and struggle to remain engaged in our digital age. During such moments, I hear my internal commentary: *This is not the type of world I want to live in. I don't want to spend the majority of my time looking at screens.*

I resist many of the changes that are happening in our digital age. Rather than a tool for enhancing communication, our devices have become a tail that is wagging us. I don't want to be wagged. Nor do I want to see others being wagged, as they mindlessly look at their phones (whether or not there is a reason for doing so). The change I resist the most is the incessant, continuous pace that our digital devices now demand. I don't want to live my life tethered to a phone. I have no interest in an always on, always available, 24/7 way of life. I shudder at the thought of sleeping with my cell phone. And I especially dislike the expectation of rapid response to every text, email, or phone call I receive. (I know all too well that my most rapid responses are rarely my best ones.) Perhaps it's my temperament and perhaps it's my age, yet I miss the days when people used to pick up the phone and call me (rather than email). Nowadays we need to schedule a phone call via email first.

What we resist, persists. Any time we experience resistance, we are being offered an invitation to listen within and ferret out what is at the root of this resistance. As I listen within to my internal conversation, I notice my resistance stemming from two sources: the first is the pressure to keep up; the second is a commitment to what I value.

I resist our growing reliance on electronic devices because it forces me to acquire skills I find difficult to learn. Right now I'm trying to figure out how to connect my desktop calendar to my phone's calendar. I know I'll soon learn how to sync my calendars, and I know once I do I'll find it beneficial to be able to do so. Yet, at the moment, I miss the ease of just writing down dates and times in a pocket calendar. I recognize that the discomfort such learning requires of me points to an opportunity for growth. Therefore, I cannot dismiss all electronic devices outright just because I find it challenging to learn about and keep up with them.

I also resist our growing reliance on electronic devices because they impinge on my, and our collective, time for reflection and rest. I want to live more mindfully—being present, attentive, and responsive to others. I notice that too much screen time leaves me distracted, reactive, and self-absorbed. As executive leadership mentor and therapist Wayne Muller reminds us in his beautiful book *Sabbath: Finding Rest, Renewal, and Delight in Our Busy Lives*:

> The theology of progress forces us to act before we are ready. We speak before we know what to say. We respond before we feel the truth of what we know. In the process, we inadvertently create suffering, heaping imprecision upon inaccuracy, until we are all buried under a mountain of misperception. But Sabbath says, Be still. Stop. There is no rush to get to the end, because we are never finished. Take time to rest, and eat, and drink, and be refreshed. And in the gentle rhythm of that refreshment, listen to the sound the heart makes as it speaks the quiet truth of what is needed.[4]

When I take the time to listen to the quiet truth of my heart, here's what I hear: I want to consciously choose where I place my attention. I want to notice what is occurring in the environment I am in. I want to use my eyes to look into others' eyes, be they friend or stranger. I want to be fully human, fully alive, not fully automated and fully distracted.

I suspect that I will always prefer to connect heart to heart rather than screen to screen, to speak face to face (or voice to voice) rather than on a social media site, to listen rather than tweet. The changes I am facing as a nondigital native in a digital age are impelling me to keep stretching beyond my comfort zone. And stretching beyond my comfort zone is a good thing for me to do. Nonetheless, the changes I am experiencing also remind me that what I most value is fully engaging in this moment and deeply engaging with those whom I encounter in it.

᙮

What experience has entered your life
that is inviting you to wake up?

Practice

This day, in the midst of experiences you find difficult or challenging, try *to open, be curious, and develop some sense of sympathy* for what is happening.

Cultivate Stillness

Pause

> What is your name—who are you—and can you find
> a way to hear the sound of the genuine in yourself?
> There are so many noises going on inside of you, so
> many echoes of all sorts, so much internalizing of the
> rumble and the traffic, the confusions, the disorders
> by which your environment is peopled that I wonder
> if you can get still enough—not quiet enough—still
> enough to hear rumbling up from your unique and
> essential idiom the sound of the genuine in you. I
> don't know if you can. But this is your assignment.
> —Howard Thurman, "The Sound of the Genuine"

Ponder

*Who are you? How does the sound of the genuine come through
to you?* As a child, Howard Thurman (1899–1981)
learned to listen to the sound of the genuine as he
walked along the beach of the Atlantic or through the
woods. Newberry Medal–winning author Elizabeth
Yates recounts a specific experience in her book, *Howard
Thurman—Portrait of a Practical Dreamer*:

The sun had disappeared behind the pines and moss-draped oaks, and the stillness that embraced the world embraced him until it seemed as if earth, river, sky, boy, shared the same pulse. Beyond the stillness and within it was a Presence that spoke to him without a voice, revealed Itself to him without a vision. Howard found himself replying, not in words that would stir silence but in wordless rapture of communion.[5]

Over the years, in my work as a professor, leadership coach, retreat facilitator, and spiritual director, I've had the privilege of listening to many people describe their specific experiences of hearing the sound of the genuine. In a recent conversation, my friend Paul told me about what he learned, many years ago, while he was out in the woods camping:

I awoke before the first signs of dawn and went out of the tent to listen to the stillness (the most silent part of the night—long after the frogs and crickets stopped their chirping). In the stillness, I then heard the lone song of a bird—no other sound in the forest. I listened very intently to that solitary voice, trying to orient myself to where it was originating. But I couldn't gain a fix on its location—it was somewhere and everywhere in that moment. Within minutes it was joined by another songbird, then another, and another until there was quite a chorus of voices. But since I had trained my ear to the original voice, I could discern it from all of the others. When the first signs of light began to seep into the forest darkness, more sounds of the morning were heard—dogs barking, cars on a nearby road, a distant plane flying overhead—all the sounds of the day began to swell up within minutes. But I could still hear the original songbird, now otherwise lost—blending amid the cacophony of sounds. I remember having the impression that I was listening to my own song of life, destined for me to follow its notes tuning into my heart throughout the day's distractions, duties, and disturbances. It was a song I had to begin with, for I wouldn't have discerned it amid the day's other sounds, only out of the stillness before the dawn.

This is *our* assignment: to get still enough to hear the sound of the genuine in us. It's immensely challenging to hear the sound of the genuine in the midst of all the activities and noises that fill our daily lives. Nonetheless, it's possible to do so *after* we have trained or attuned our ear to its original voice. In issuing this assignment, Thurman is inviting us to discover the places and practices that prove to be most conducive for us to get still and attune our ears. For some of us, it may be walking on the beach or camping in the woods; for others, it may be staying indoors and gazing out the window. It's not so much where we go or what we do; what's most important is that we do it. Otherwise, as Thurman admonishes, "we will spend our days on the ends of strings that somebody else pulls."[6]

What do you do or where do you go to get
still enough to listen to the sound of the
genuine in you? What helps you train your
ear to discern the sound of the genuine
from all the other sounds in your life?

Practice

Today, experiment with ways of cultivating stillness. If possible, begin by listening to the stillness before the dawn. As you move through the activities of your day, experiment with returning to stillness by pausing to take a few deep breaths before turning your attention to the next activity. At the end of the day, carve out some time to return to stillness before going to sleep.

Heed the Whispers

Pause

Into the Interior

I am your whispered voice

your inside voice

your interior voice

your unheard voice

your unspoken voice

your unvoiced voice

your unspeakable voice

I am your heart's voice and your heartless voice

your deepest voice

under layers of living & speaking

the voice of your buried life

your invisible life

your silent life

your unknown life

your unopened life

your unrealized life

the undiscovered life that no one sees

not even your lover

not even yourself

If you will listen to me
if you will lend me the ear
of your mind
and of your bent heart
if you will heed my whisperings …
heed my whisperings …
heed my whisperings …
heed my whisperings …
    —Lawrence Ferlinghetti[7]

Ponder

I awoke in the middle of the night. Something was beckoning for my attention, and I knew it would be futile to try to get back to sleep. Instead, I got out of bed, went into the living room, and began to meditate. Before long, I experienced a tide of energy surging through me. As I sat, I felt as if I had plugged into a power source whose wattage far exceeded my normal charge. It reminded of me of a line from one of my favorite poems, "Last Night, As I Was Sleeping," where the poet Antonio Machado dreams that a spring is breaking out in his heart. This wasn't the first time I had experienced the sensation of a spring breaking out in my heart. However, the force of the spring inside my heart that night was particularly strong. It could not be ignored. It was the sound of my deepest voice, the voice of my unrealized self, confirming that it was time to take action.

For weeks before that particular night, I had begun work on this book and was trying to discern what was being asked of me with this project. Since the publication of my first book, *Conversation—The Sacred Art: Practicing Presence in an Age of Distraction*, I have been giving presentations in various settings. I've met more and more leaders who are looking for ways to deepen engagement in conversations about topics that are difficult to talk about in public, especially workplace, settings. My first book drew upon spiritual teachings and practices from many faith traditions for enriching conversations. I recognized that the religious language I'd used in writing *Conversation—The Sacred Art* might prove problematic in some public settings. Therefore, in response to the expressed needs of these leaders, I felt a calling to write a book for deepening our engagement in conversation without using explicitly religious language.

As I considered moving in this direction, I spoke with a number of colleagues and friends about it. I noticed how their voices landed in two contradictory camps: the first set focused on greed, the second on need. Those in the greed camp assumed there would be little to no interest in a book about deepening engagement, especially in corporate workplace settings, unless it resulted in a profitable bottom line. On the other side of the spectrum were those who work in such settings and report feeling numb and overwhelmed as a result. They are looking for concrete, practical ways to increase their engagement and overall satisfaction. As I participated in these conversations I listened to the voices within me that emerged in response: the voices of my emotions, my intellect, my experience, my will, and my ego.

The voice of my emotions was the loudest, especially the voice of my fear. The voice of our fears is not only loud, but it is also hard to ignore. Its critical messages clamor for our attention. Fear's refrains are repetitive and predictable. I'd heard them fester within me before: *What do you know about corporate life? You've spent most of your life teaching in colleges and universities. You've never worked in a corporation. You've only studied and taught about organizational development or conducted research in various corporations. What would you have to offer them?*

Although quieter in volume, the voice of my intellect disagreed with the voice of my fear. I knew as a scholar and a researcher that I could help and had helped many organizational leaders frame meaningful conversations. The voice of my lived experience echoed that of my intellect—providing ample evidence from over twenty-five years of teaching, designing, and facilitating conversations—that it was possible to prepare and equip participants to engage more mindfully in conversation. The voice of my will was unequivocal: *You can do this, Diane. This would be a great stretch for you. It would be good to work some new muscles and write in ways that are not explicitly religious.* The voice of my ego (which I tend to listen to with caution, given its wily ways) reminded me that I had something unique to offer.

All of us have this collection of voices that fill and commingle in our consciousness: the echoes of the external voices of other people and the array of internal voices of our emotions, our intellect, our lived experience, our will, and our ego in response. In making any decision, we benefit from taking the time to become cognizant of them; that is, to notice and name the messages they are conveying and to assess their truthfulness. Yet whenever we are trying to discern what to do next, the process doesn't end there.

As the poet Lawrence Ferlinghetti notes in "Into the Interior," there is a voice that is even deeper than all these external and internal voices. *It is our heart's voice and our heartless voice, our deepest voice under layers of living and speaking.* The sound of our interior voice is more akin to a whisper. It need not shout (although it may on occasion). More often, our heart's most genuine messages are subtle, rather than direct. Their volume is often closer to mute and experienced energetically (as they were for me that particular night in meditation). At times, we may experience our deepest voice as a felt sense—that is, a stirring within us accompanied by sensations of warmth, peace, and comfort. The messages of our deepest voice may also be expressed through an image that seems to spontaneously emerge for us while engaged in a conversation, in reflection, or in a dream. Regardless of how we hear it, this is what I know to be true of its messages. We know we are hearing our deepest voice when we feel enlivened, more than excited by it; when we feel drawn, rather than driven, to undertake an action; and when the message lingers and lasts, rather than evaporating and eluding us.

It is this deeper voice, most akin to a whisper, to which we need to keep listening regularly, frequently, often.

What whisper is asking to be heeded
in your life at this time?

Practice

This day, heed what is whispering in the depths of your being. Carve out some time to quietly attend to the myriad voices in your life. What are the external voices saying? What are your internal voices saying—that is, the voices of your emotions, intellect, lived experience, will, and ego? Where do you experience resonance or dissonance between these voices and the deepest voice within you?

Shift Your Vision

Pause

> I began to look more closely, not at things but at a world closer to myself, looking from an inner place to one further within, instead of clinging to the movement of sight toward the world outside.
>
> —Jacques Lusseyran, *And There Was Light: The Extraordinary Memoir of a Blind Hero of the French Resistance in World War II*

What we call "seeing" is generally a reflection of our inner dialogue, which is constant and unceasing. Our inner dialogue tends to support our particular worldview, our image of ourself, and our subjective beliefs. We know too much; we can name and provide a label for everything under the sun. We have our own agendas, our predisposed attitudes, and our own cultural biases. We rarely see the world in a fresh way or question the numerous and often unconscious filters that influence the nature of our perception. Moments of real seeing are beyond the labeling propensity of the mind, beyond what we think we know.

Seeing is a step into the unknown and requires
some degree of intention and awakening.
>—David Ulrich, *The Widening Stream:*
>*The Seven Stages of Creativity*

Ponder

"My eyes, where are my eyes?" was the first thing
Jacques Lusseyran asked when he regained consciousness. The last thing he remembered was jumping up and
running out to recess. On the way, one of his classmates
ran into him, causing Lusseyran to lose his balance. He
hit his head on a sharp corner of his teacher's desk. The
arm of his spectacles lodged deep into his right eye and
it tore away. The blow was so hard that it caused sym-
pathetic opthalmia in his left eye. At age seven, Lusseyran became completely and permanently blind. He
recounts in his memoir, *And There Was Light*:

> It was a great surprise to find myself blind, and being
> blind was not at all as I imagined it. Nor was it as the
> people around me seemed to think it. They told me
> that to be blind was not to see. Yet how was I to believe
> them when I saw?... I saw light and went on seeing it
> though I was blind.... I was not light myself, I knew
> that, but I bathed in it as an element which blind-
> ness had suddenly brought much closer. I could feel
> light rising, spreading, resting on objects, giving them
> form, then leaving them.... Since it was not I who was

making the light, since it came to me from outside, it would never leave me. I was only a passageway, a vestibule for this brightness. The seeing eye was in me.[8]

Throughout his memoir, Lusseyran describes how he learned to pay attention to *the seeing eye* within him. He noticed that the light faded, almost to the point of disappearing, every time he was afraid, angry, or impatient. He observed, "When I was playing with my small companions, if I suddenly grew anxious to win, to be first at all costs, then all at once I could see nothing. Literally I went into fog or smoke. I could no longer afford to be jealous or unfriendly, because, as soon as I was, a bandage came down over my eyes, and I was bound hand and foot and cast aside. All at once a black hole opened, and I was helpless inside it. But when I was happy and serene, approached people with confidence and thought well of them, I was rewarded with light."[9] His growing reliance on this new way of seeing taught him how to live.

At the age of thirty-three, photographer David Ulrich lost his capacity to see with his right eye after the fractured tip of a small branch struck him while he was chopping wood. He recounts in his book, *The Widening Stream: The Seven Stages of Creativity*, that this horrific accident yielded an unexpected blessing:

In losing the sight of my eye, I learned to depend to a great extent on efforts toward self-awareness and connecting with my own body and feelings. I clearly observed how the objects of my perception registered their impression on my being and stimulated widely varying inner sensations and feelings. Although I do not fully understand this process, perhaps the larger potential of seeing is found in these moments of self-awareness and the recognition that all impressions we receive register themselves within us. Seeing comes from within ourselves, not from the vague "out there" of the outer world.[10]

The seeing eye is in all of us. Lusseyran and Ulrich discovered another way of seeing, and knowing, beyond that of our visual senses. Yet, we don't have to become blind in order to do so. Rather, we can practice shifting our vision from merely *looking at* the surface of things to *looking into* them from a vantage point *deep within* us. Instead of increasing the amount of time we spend *taking in* more images and information with our eyes each day, what if we instead increased our attentiveness to what we are *receiving deep within* us? We may end up being far more selective about what we expose our outer eyes to as a result.

⚬

What environments help you to shift your vision?
Where do you go, or what do you
do, to increase your capacity to see
with the entirety of your being?

Practice

This day, take time to look deeply into someone or something. As you behold this person or object, notice the
inner sensations and feelings you receive as you do so.

Notice What Nourishes

Pause

A man is a method, a progressive arrangement; a selecting principle, gathering his like to him wherever he goes. He takes only his own out of the multiplicity that sweeps and circles round him … Those facts, words, persons, which dwell in his memory without his being able to say why, remain because they have a relation to him not less real for being as yet unapprehended. They are symbols of value to him as they can interpret parts of his consciousness which he would vainly seek words for in the conventional images of books and other minds. What attracts my attention shall have it … A few anecdotes, a few traits of character, manners, face, a few incidents, have an emphasis in your memory out of all proportion to their apparent significance if you measure them by the ordinary standards. They relate to your gift. Let them have their weight, and do not reject them and cast about for illustrations and facts

more usual in literature. What your heart thinks
great, is great. The soul's emphasis is always right.
> —Ralph Waldo Emerson, *The Spiritual Emerson:*
> *Essential Works by Ralph Waldo Emerson*

Ponder

What attracts my attention shall have it. When I was a
child, I loved to sit at my desk and gaze out the window. It was there that I crafted my notepads. Long
before the days of sticky notes, I prided myself on
how cost-effectively (and beautifully) I could create
gently ascending spiral stacks of multicolored paper.
I remember spending hours cutting the pages just so,
assembling the right number of pieces, selecting the
arrangement of colors, and then gluing them together.
What made it especially gratifying was knowing I was
creating gifts I could share.

When I wasn't creating, I was reading. I would miss
a lot of things in order to read, even school. I was
reminded once again that I had the coolest mother in
the world that day in fourth grade when I complained
of a stomachache. I had asked her if I could stay home
to tend it and she readily agreed. It was amazing how
quickly the ache in my stomach ceased as I cracked
open that book on Abraham Lincoln. Later that afternoon, my mother brought me a candy bar. She knew, as
did I, that there are some days we just need to finish a
good book.

While I relished my time in solitude most of all, I did enjoy time with others, especially if we were playing school. I was blessed to have a younger sister and friends who were willing to do so even after returning from a full day at school. What was particularly admirable about their willingness was that no one ever got to be the teacher but me. In truth, I don't recall how many times we played school. It may have only been a handful (I mean, honestly, how much fun could that have been for them?). Yet, it was these incidents, however few, that hold immense significance for me to this day.

Each of our lives is filled with memories. As psychologists remind us, our memories are constructed rather than representative of what actually occurred. Some memories nourish and invigorate us; other memories trouble and dismay us. As Emerson underscores, our most enduring, nourishing memories reflect our truest self, our essence, and point to our gifts. That is why it is so important for us to pay attention to *what our heart thinks great*. On occasion, we may be surprised by how something or someone captivates our attention and impels us to reminisce. I vividly remember the time I heard a beloved song from my childhood, *This little light of mine, I'm going to let it shine,* and how this constellation of memories of me creating, reading, and playing school reappeared.

What does that particular constellation of activities that my heart thought was great *then* reveal about my gifts in the here and *now*? It reminds me that I value activities that reconnect me with the creative light within, books that enable me to be enlightened by the wisdom of others, and opportunities to share my light and love of learning with others. While I no longer create notepads, I still enjoy sitting at my desk, working on creative projects, and gazing out the window. As an educator and writer, I try to create evocative presentations and essays. Now, as then, I experience immense gratification at the prospect of offering what I am designing as a gift for others. While I no longer skip school to stay home and read, I have grown to appreciate being self-employed and setting my own schedule. This allows me ample time to read, reflect, and work at my own pace. And while I no longer play school, my aim is to offer playful presentations, workshops, and retreats that participants would choose to attend even after a full day at work or school.

⚬

What memories captivate your attention?
Is there a particular song, book, movie, or activity
that you were especially attracted to as a child?
How does what you derived joy from then
relate to your gifts in the here and now?

Practice

Throughout this day, pay attention to what your heart thinks is great. It may be something as simple as drinking a cup of coffee or listening to one of your favorite songs while you work. At the close of the day, take a few moments to reflect upon all the activities and people your heart thought were great.

Clean Your
Compass Often

Pause

Clean Your Compass Often

Sometimes, when you think
you should be going this way,
the needle trembles, points
ever so slightly to that way.
Sometimes even the opposite
direction. Oddly, the compass
sometimes seems to make a sound,
as if ticking, measuring time's
relentless gift.

You think you know.
Sometimes you do.
But if you want your life
to be alive for you,
allow yourself to be
surprised.

Make time to sit
with your compass.
Preferably daily.
You need a good cloth;
soft, and well-worn.
Perhaps you can sit
with the compass
in your upturned palm.
Shut your eyes. Or not.
Maybe put it next to your bed.
It might encourage
your dreams to suggest
destinations.

They say a compass
is both teacher and student;
it gets to know you,
what serves you best,
if you make friends with it.
They say it's like *as below
so above,* and the opposite.
They say a clean compass
can lead to mountaintops;
equally, maybe even more
importantly it can lead
to vales where shadows
hide gold.

Your job is simple.
The compass.
Your breath.
You.
—Jennifer (Jinks) Hoffmann

Ponder

For months, I had had a hard time swallowing. My throat often ached. It frequently felt as if there were something stuck in it. Yet, I knew the symptoms I was experiencing had nothing whatsoever to do with a virus or a cold. I knew it was my body's compass trying to get my attention.

For months, my husband had seen me struggling with the new set of responsibilities I had taken on at the college where I had been teaching for more than five years. I had been asked to develop a project for deepening students' spirituality. In collaboration with a gifted team, I had written a grant and the college had been awarded $1.5 million to fund it. As a result, my focus had had to turn from teaching to administration. Although I had never envisioned myself as or aspired to be an administrator in higher education, I was willing to do so temporarily in order to do what I truly felt called to do, which was teach. During the first year of the project's implementation, I pushed myself to the point of exhaustion. All the while, I kept hoping that if the project succeeded (which it did), I would stand a better chance of securing a permanent teaching position (which I didn't). My husband and I had both agreed that if a permanent job offer were not forthcoming, it would be time for me to move on.

For months, I had had a series of recurring dreams involving roads. The following was the most memorable:

> I am on a freeway. It is dark. I have an intuitive feeling that I am approaching a busy city. I'm not worried about finding my way in the city. However, I am concerned about finding my way back from the city, as there are no signs on the freeway to guide me. I am mindful of the need to remember the roads I have taken so that I can eventually find my way back when I choose to return. I am also conscious of the need to slow down the speed at which the car is traveling. As I approach a fork in the road, I intend to go right, but the car veers left. As this occurs, I am all the more conscious of the need to pay attention to the roads I have taken so that I can find my way back. My anxiety is less about finding my way to the destination; it is more about finding my way home. I know I don't want to stay long at whatever the destination is. Instead, I want to get home …

For months, I had been cleaning my compass often. The needles from the image in my dreams, the conversations with my husband, and the lump in my throat all pointed in the same direction. I was no longer on the right road.

It was time to turn and find my way home. I eventually resigned from my position at the college.

In her book, *Finding Your Own North Star: Claiming the Life You Were Meant to Live*, sociologist and life coach Martha Beck offers some tips on finding our way home that I have adapted into questions:

- Which persons, places, or things do you find yourself drawn to?
- Which persons, places, or things increase your energy?
- With whom and in what environments do you feel socially adept, confident, and at ease?
- What types of information are you able to retain with ease?
- Which activities do you find so absorbing that you lose track of time?

Feeling drawn to something rather than driven, energized rather than drained, at ease rather than ill at ease, absorbed rather than detached are all indicators that our compass's needle is pointing toward our true north. Beck offers two additional readings she recommends we take when we find ourselves in the midst of particularly challenging circumstances:

- Is your health better than usual, even in spite of additional exertion?
- Does your sense of joy persist, even in the face of fear, sadness, or challenge?[11]

It is painful to disengage from those people, places, or activities that once enlivened us yet no longer do. On occasion, I still wonder what the last ten years of my life would have been like had I stayed at the college. I loved working with the students there. My dream had always been to teach undergraduates, and I continue to miss being a regular part of a campus community. Over time, I've grown to accept that I may never be permanently employed at a college or university. Yet that has not stopped me from teaching. I will always be a teacher. I don't have to give up that part of my dream. In relinquishing and mourning the previous version of my dream, I have slowly gained freedom. Freedom to explore the writing I want to do (rather than what my discipline dictates), freedom to develop new venues for teaching and learning (rather than a traditional class-room), and freedom to build relationships with students and colleagues in an assortment of settings (rather than concentrating my energy on just one).

Cleaning our compass not only often requires discipline. It also requires courage. Perhaps most of all, it requires encouragement. We can't do it on our own. We need others to help us decipher the meaning of the needle when it trembles.

∽

Have you ever had to disengage from people, places, or activities that once enlivened you?

What happened? Who was involved?
What impact did the experience have on your life?
Who are the people, places, or activities
you find yourself drawn to at this time?

Practice

Today, notice the persons, places, and activities that increase your energy and to which you feel drawn. At the end of the day, name with whom and in what environments you felt most at ease.

Honor Your Grief

Pause

Gathering Blossoms

Where will you plant your grief-seeds? We need ground
to scrape and hoe, not the sky of unspecified desire.
> —Jellaladin Rumi

Loss rose from her garden,
spoke gently between plantings,

conversed softly of death
and dianthus, of despair and dahlias.

Guided by grief, heart in dust,
mind in memory, tears fell, sank,

into the loam of soul. Each turn
of hoe, every scrape into ground,

became honorable labor, honorable
in its intention to transform.

Digging, unearthing, seeing,
she beheld her father, followed

his image as he tended to tea rose
and tulip, dianthus and dahlia;

she watched his eyes brighten
as he handled, cupped, the stuff of life.

Buried in darkness, stirrings
pushed where seedlings emerged,

where buds reached for the sky, grew
with the specified desire to live!

Blossoms rose from her garden;
they swirled in crinolines of green,

delighted in bonnets of petalled-softness,
as if to say, *Dance with us, laugh,
we're your grief-seeds—transformed!*
     —Jeannie E. Roberts

Ponder

My maternal grandmother was renowned for her gardening. When someone took her picture, she loved to be photographed in her flower garden. Earlier in her life, she had tended many vegetables during the years she and my grandfather lived on their farm in central Minnesota. It was on that farm that their second child and only son, Donald, died in my grandmother's arms from whooping cough. He was four at the time. It was on that farm that my mother, Rosemary, was born the following year. While she was a child, my mother doesn't recall her parents ever speaking about her brother's death. What she does remember is that after she was diagnosed with polio at age five, her parents sold their farm and bought a house in the nearest city, St. Cloud. There, my grandmother's flowers blossomed.

Each of us experiences grief over the course of our lives. It may be the seeds from the loss of loved ones, the loss of our health, the loss of a job, the loss of our home, the loss of our youth, or the loss of a dream for our life. Whatever our particular medley of seeds, psychologists speak about the importance of honoring our grief rather than denying or striving to overcome it. How we do that is unique to each of us, although the terrain we travel may be similar.[12]

I never had the chance to ask my grandmother about how she tended the seeds of her grief because she died when I was nine. Ironically, her death was the first loss I experienced in my life. All I can recount is the blossoms I witnessed. Like her flowers, she was deeply rooted. I know she was a woman of prayer. Although she never spoke about her way of praying, I could feel the energy of her prayer emanate from her bedroom. It was my favorite spot in her home. I used to love sleeping in there and the time I could spend there alone, gazing at the twinkling candles above her prie deux kneeler. I have since learned from other family members that the loss of her son never embittered her; rather, her capacity to love became all the more tender. I too can recall the tenderness in her eyes, and the hint of sadness at their center. Grief is like that—although the anguish may lessen over time, an ache still lingers.

Whether or not we are gardeners, each of us holds seeds of grief in the palms of our hands. Some of us may keep our hands tightly clenched, preferring to pretend those seeds are not there. Some of us just want to get rid of them—to throw them out into the sky or the nearest receptacle. Yet the process of honoring our grief invites us to examine the seeds from both the losses in our lives (deaths, illnesses, jobs, and dreams) and the endings (of relationships, of work, of various life stages).

Anthropologist Angeles Arrien offers us a process for working with our grief seeds she calls honorable closure. Honorable closure is based on a ritual practiced among indigenous people to mark endings, to acknowledge the impact of our experiences, and to glean wisdom from them.[13] It consists of four questions:

- What am I grateful for from the experience?
- How was I positively impacted?
- How was I stretched or challenged?
- Is there anything I need to say or do to feel complete?

Throughout her lifetime, my mother has displayed a picture of the brother she never met in the living room. I love that picture and make a point to gaze at it whenever I visit her. I can't imagine anything more painful than having my child die in my arms. I don't know how

I would have survived it. I am grateful that my grandparents had the courage to love another child after such an immense loss. The impact of their love shaped my mother in indelible ways. Every time we are with our mother, she never ceases to remind us (my two younger sisters and me, and now our children) that we are the biggest blessings in her life. My grandparents' steadfast commitment to keep reaching out in love in the midst of their loss challenges me to do the same. I can only hope that my life is worthy of their example.

Out of your grief, what have you created
or what do you hope to create?

Practice

Today, reflect upon an ending in your life. To the extent that you feel ready, consider what you feel grateful for in that experience; how you were positively impacted; how you were stretched or challenged; and whether there is anything more you need to do or say in response.

Part Two

Engaging
One Another

Abandon Your Hat

Pause

The Rush of Mystery

The air is vengeful
despite the radiant sky.
Normally placid sea curls
have become white-topped
fiery jumpers, and rush menacingly
towards today's few walkers.
There are not many
as faithful as I.
How can I love
only when life is gentle?
The rush of Mystery today
frightens a little,
and asks for steady feet
on bone-chilling sand,
and against gale-like winds.
We regulars have abandoned
our hats.
Leaving our heads bare
feels almost sacred today.

—Jennifer (Jinks) Hoffmann

Ponder

The opening poem reminds me of one of my favorite stories about two walkers told by Christian theologian and mystic Evelyn Underhill. The first walker, "No-Eyes," is concerned with getting from point A to point B as efficiently as possible. He doesn't notice what's on the side of the road, nor does he feel the caress of the wind on his skin. The second walker, "Eyes," walks the same terrain and "it is a perpetual revelation of beauty and wonder. The sunlight inebriates him, the winds delight him, the very effort of the journey is a joy. Magic presences throng the roadside, or cry salutations to him from the hidden field. The rich world through which he moves lies in the foreground of his consciousness; and it gives up new secrets to him at every step."[1] The poet Jinks Hoffmann speaks about those who walk in the world as "Eyes" does—beholding all they encounter with awe and wonder.

My father is a walker. He walks daily wherever and whenever possible. He taught my sisters and me the value of walking for the sake of fitness and forging connections. If he wants to have a heart-to-heart talk with you, he invites you for a walk. He seems to know what creativity researchers have confirmed: if you're stuck, go out and take a walk and let your subconscious work things through. In spite of his example, for a large part of my life I preferred to drive rather than walk. Walking requires exertion and I don't like to sweat. Walking also takes more time, and I, like "No-Eyes," typically want to get to my destination as quickly as possible.

My conversion from rider to walker was gradual. Initially, my walking was solely motivated by its physical benefits. I noticed that I felt better on the days that I got twenty to thirty minutes of fresh air and sunlight—especially during the dark days of late fall and winter. However, if it was rainy, windy, or snowy, I stayed inside. By staying indoors, I didn't have to expose myself to the risks of a woman walking alone or my fear of encountering the many dogs in our neighborhood. Suffice it to say that I would never choose to walk *on bone-chilling sand against gale-like winds* or follow a path filled with *vengeful air*. Nonetheless, I relished the thought of finding myself among the faithful few, like the poet and my father, who walk in all conditions.

Walking in all conditions challenges us to practice opening our eyes and looking closely—especially at those aspects of our current reality that are not favorable, comfortable, or gentle. It's difficult to see clearly and steady our feet in the midst of life's mysterious and bewildering circumstances. Yet, rather than analyzing how the weather got to be the way it is or clinging to that which covers us, what if we, like Jinks Hoffmann, considered abandoning our hats and baring our heads instead?

Clinging to our hats tends to obscure our view of current reality. We stay absorbed in our heads, mired in the inner chatter of our thoughts and analysis. Abandoning our hats invites us to turn our attention to what is presently going on. As management consultant Robert Fritz points out in his book, *The Path of Least Resistance: Learning to Become the Creative Force in Your Own Life*, "Some people avoid an accurate recognition of current reality by continually analyzing how current reality got to be the way it is. The question *How did things get to be the way they are?* is a different question from *What is presently going on?* Many people confuse the two questions, and so spend time futilely theorizing or explaining to themselves how they got to be where they are."[2]

Like my conversion from driving to walking, our capacity to abandon our hats and bare our heads tends to be gradual and continual rather than immediate and once and for all. Each step we take on our journey invites us to loosen the grip on our hats (and our agendas) a little more and focus on what is being revealed in the present moment. Although we may find ourselves walking on terrain we would never have chosen to traverse, the more that we can bare our heads, the fuller and more unobstructed our view can be. It takes a great deal of courage to bare our heads in the midst of vengeful conditions. That is why, as my father taught me, it helps to invite others to join us on a walk. They can point out sights and invite insights we might otherwise miss.

I now try to walk daily and in all conditions. My husband often accompanies me. This past summer, I extended a number of invitations to our young adult son, Ryan, and our niece, Alexis, to join me for a walk. They declined. I understand. Their conversion from driving to walking has not yet begun.

> What is an inclement condition
> in your life at present in which you
> find it difficult to abandon your hat?
> What are the assumptions, expectations, or
> agendas that keep you from baring your head?

Practice

Today, when you encounter a challenge, take a walk. It may be as brief as getting up from your desk to get a cup of tea or going outside to walk around the block. As you walk, imagine yourself abandoning your hat as you identify whatever assumptions, expectations, or agendas you would like to release in order to bare your head and begin anew.

Open to What Is Unfolding

Pause

Introductions

Some of what we love
we stumble upon—
a purse of gold thrown on the road,
a poem, a friend, a great song.

And more
discloses itself to us—
a well among green hazels,
a nut thicket—
when we are worn out searching
for something quite different.

And more
comes to us, carried
as carefully
as a bright cup of water,
as new bread.
        —Moya Cannon

Ponder

This poem, "Introductions" by Moya Cannon, seemed to be waiting to introduce itself to me the afternoon following my lunch with a friend I'll refer to as Peter. I met Peter more than a decade ago when he and I were both teaching at the same college. Although his office was right next to mine, we didn't immediately become friends. Like many academics, he often seemed more interested in hearing himself talk than in listening to what I had to say. It wasn't until he knocked on the door of my office one morning and invited me to lunch that our friendship began. That day, I was introduced to another dimension of Peter. I witnessed his willingness to be vulnerable.

Peter and I were not encouraged to stumble upon anything. Instead, we were raised to set goals, go after what we wanted, and make things happen. At the time we first met for lunch, we also shared another commonality: we were worn out from searching. Peter told me that day how he was searching for a personal place of belonging. He described how he'd spent his twenties in graduate school, been married and then divorced. I, who at the time had been happily married for almost twenty years, was also searching for a place of belonging—a professional one. I, too, had spent my twenties in graduate school. At thirty, I gave birth to my first and only child. After that, I had wanted to teach part time. Given that it's all but impossible to find a part-time, tenure-track position, my career subsequently became that of a "road scholar"—teaching a course or two at a college or university on a semester-to-semester or year-to-year basis. By the time Peter and I became friends, I had been teaching at the same institution for five years and no offers for a permanent part-time position had been forthcoming. I was feeling stuck and demoralized. As our friendship grew, Peter became an important conversation partner as I tried to figure out what to do next. I eventually resigned from the college where we were teaching and began a career as an independent educator and consultant. Since then, Peter also began teaching at another university. We've kept in touch and try to meet for lunch whenever he is in town.

At our most recent lunch, I was happy to hear about Peter's promotion to associate professor, the grant he had received for his sabbatical, and the two books he had been invited to write (not to mention the array of leadership roles he's taken on in his field). I then told him about the new book I was working on, the film project I had just begun producing, and the other creative endeavors that filled my life. All the while, I wanted to inquire about how his search for a personal place of belonging was going. Yet that particular day it no longer felt like the most helpful thing to do.

Instead, I told Peter about a guiding principle I had recently been introduced to by the Buddhist psychologist Jack Kornfield in his book *The Wise Heart: A Guide to the Universal Teachings of Buddhist Psychology*. The gist of it is learning to open ourselves more fully to what is currently happening in our lives. Rather than focusing on the results we seek, Kornfield advises that we "give our best to the process, create what we can, and trust the larger process of life itself. We can plan, care for, tend, and respond. But we cannot control. Instead we take a breath, and open to what is unfolding, where we are. This is a profound shift, from holding on, to letting go."[3]

We talked about the implications this sensibility might have for our lives. And as we did, I noticed something begin to shift within me. During the remainder of our conversation, I no longer felt a need to help Peter figure out how or where to find his personal place of belonging.

In truth, I still wish I could arrange the universe so that Peter soon finds a well-suited partner. I know how much he'd like to remarry and start a family. I also know how much he'd like for me to receive an offer for a permanent teaching position. Nonetheless, I am slowly learning to savor what I stumble upon, to pay attention to where I am, and to be on the lookout for whatever is trying to introduce itself to me, be it *a well, a nut thicket, a bright cup of water, new bread,* or a colleague who knocks on my office door.

∽

What is disclosing itself to you or
unfolding for you at this moment?

Practice

Today, cultivate a stance of anticipation, being ever ready for an introduction to something or someone that will disclose itself to you.

Turn to Wonder

Pause

Moses was keeping the flock of his father-in-law
Jethro, the priest of Midian; he led his flock beyond
the wilderness, and came to Horeb, the mountain
of God. There the angel of the Lord appeared to
him in a flame of fire out of a bush; he looked, and
the bush was blazing, yet it was not consumed.
Then Moses said, "I must turn aside and look at this
great sight, and see why the bush is not burned up."
When the Lord saw that he had turned aside to see,
God called to him out of the bush, "Moses, Moses!"
And he said, "Here I am." Then he said, "Come no
closer! Remove the sandals from your feet, for the
place on which you are standing is holy ground."

—Exodus 3:1–5, *New Revised Standard Version*

When the going gets rough, turn to wonder.
If you feel judgmental, or defensive, ask
yourself, "I wonder what brought her to this
belief?" "I wonder what he's feeling right
now?" "I wonder what my reaction teaches me

about myself?" Set aside judgment to listen to others—and to yourself—more deeply.

—Center for Courage and Renewal's
Circles of Trust Touchstones

Ponder

The story of Moses's calling is one of my favorites. It never ceases to amaze me how the meanings we derive from our most familiar and beloved stories—both the ones we tell about our own lives and the ones we read about or hear from others—lend themselves to new interpretations. For the first fifty years of my life, I was a Moses wannabe. I wanted to hear my name being called by a divine voice, "Diane, Diane!" with a clear mandate regarding what I was supposed to do next. Yet, in the past year or two, I have found my attention riveted to Moses's decision to "turn aside and look at this great sight, and see why the bush is not burned up."[4] Moses's note to self and to me: pause and turn to wonder.

We must turn aside and look …

Each of us encounters bushes ablaze yet not consumed over the course of our lives. Yet, let's face it. Most of us don't want to take a closer look, especially at whatever we find frightening. Our tendency is to do our best to avoid those people, places, and situations that arouse our fear. It's far easier, and far safer, to keep moving in the direction we're headed rather than to veer off course and examine the surprising and unsettling situations in our lives.

We must turn aside and look ...

The pressure we feel to keep moving ahead in our current age is immense. We spend our days constantly attuning to everything without fully concentrating on anything. As writer and consultant Linda Stone observes, we live in a state of CPA—continuous partial attention—the term she coined to describe our high alert, always on, anywhere, anytime, anyplace behavior. A longtime tech executive, Stone acknowledges that, like so many things, "in small doses, continuous partial attention can be a very functional behavior. However, in a 24/7, always-on world, continuous partial attention used as our dominant attention mode contributes to a feeling of overwhelm, overstimulation and to a sense of being unfulfilled. We are so accessible, we're inaccessible."[5] Our capacity to turn and look and focus on surprising sights is diminishing. That will have to wait until our next vacation.

We must turn aside and look ...

Nonetheless, it is imperative that we do so. Taking time to pause and turn our attention has innumerable benefits, as CEO and executive development expert Kevin Cashman explains in his book *The Pause Principle: Step Back to Lead Forward.* Pausing—that is, consciously and intentionally stepping back and reflecting upon what is going on within us and outside of us—increases the likelihood that we will turn from ...

- A presumption of knowing and expertise to listening and learning.

- The status quo to curiosity, exploration, synthesis, and innovation.
- Heroic, unchallenged ideas to collaborative, constructive engagement.[6]

We, like Moses, encounter unforeseen events that seemingly interfere with our daily routines at home and work. There's the family member who is being difficult. There's the client or customer who isn't satisfied with our service or product. There's the coworker or colleague who takes credit for our work. Rather than pause and turn our attention to trying to better understand them, we tend to turn and avoid these folks. Yet, what if we took a page from Moses's playbook?

The next time we encounter people we perceive to be difficult—family members, customers, or coworkers—what if we paused and intentionally turned to wonder by engaging them in a conversation? In so doing, we run the risk that they may say something that will push our buttons. Yet instead of turning to judgment and annoyance, and thinking to ourselves, *What an idiot*, what if we instead paused and turned and asked ourselves, "I wonder what leads him or her to that conclusion?" If the time seems right, we might even ask the person about it. As Kevin Cashman reminds us, questioning is perhaps the most powerful pause of all. He encourages us to turn our focus from having all the answers to offering questions that engage others, our enterprises, and ourselves in optimal discovery.[7]

When things get difficult ... when the going gets rough ... when the unexpected happens ... what if we turned from judgment and engaged our curiosity by considering these questions:

- I wonder, What brought her to that opinion?
- I wonder, What's it like for her to feel that way?
- I wonder, What is he feeling right now?
- I wonder, What does my reaction teach me about myself?[8]

Who is someone in your life with whom
you could practice turning to wonder?

Practice

This day, turn to wonder and try to discover something more about each of the people with whom you interact. It may be trying to notice something new in a person who is very familiar to you, looking for something to appreciate in a person you find odd or difficult, or engaging someone with whom you don't typically interact in a conversation.

Polish the Mirror

Pause

> Just as polishing transforms a mineral or stone into
> a reflection object, the human being who can regu-
> larly wipe clean the mirror of awareness will begin
> to reflect the light of being itself.... If we could clear
> the inner mirror, the light of Being would be reflected
> outwardly as light, as light pouring out of our eyes.
> —Kabir Helminski, *Living Presence: A Sufi*
> *Way to Mindfulness and the Essential Self*

> What you have to attempt—to be yourself. What
> you have to pray for—to become a mirror in which,
> according to the degree of purity of heart you have
> attained, the greatness of life will be reflected.
> —Dag Hammarskjöld, *Markings*

Ponder

I was the last person to arrive for dinner at the retreat
house. I was tired and eager to wrap up dinner and
the required getting to know other participants before
entering into silence for the remainder of the weekend.
From the door, I saw some fifteen retreatants gathered

in the dining room. I felt a sense of immediate relief when I saw Bonnie standing among them with her signature slightly upturned smile. The warmth of her gaze seemed to follow me as I was introduced to the other participants. When my attention turned to her, she gently nodded and responded, "Oh, I know Diane." Over the past couple of years, Bonnie and I have seen each other regularly—both on retreats and through our service on this retreat center's board. Regardless of the setting or occasion, her keen attentiveness never ceases to amaze me. In meetings, she consistently takes time to drink in what others have to say. I love to look her way when I speak and take note of the delight-filled expression that appears on her face. I often feel as if I must be saying something truly insightful. Yet, I also love to look her way while on silent retreat and observe her countenance. Whether Bonnie is in conversation or in silence, what I most notice about her is the light that pours forth from her eyes. I so want to bask and linger in that light. As the retreat drew to a close on Sunday morning, I noticed Maya Angelou's words echoing in my heart: "I've learned that people will forget what you said, people will forget what you did, but people will never forget how you made them feel."[9] And I knew who it was that helped me to remember.

I will never forget how people like Bonnie make me feel. Conversely, I will never forget how people like Marilyn make me feel, either. Over the past decade, I've attended conferences and participated in meetings with Marilyn (a pseudonym). I have been introduced to her on numerous occasions. Nonetheless, whenever I see her, I consistently feel a need to reintroduce myself to her because her facial expression conveys that she can't quite place me on her mattering map. Moreover, whenever we speak, she seems to be looking right past me.

We all have Bonnies in our life, and we have all interacted with one or more Marilyns. I suspect that regardless of whom Bonnie interacts with, they experience light pouring forth from her eyes. And, perhaps light pours forth from Marilyn's eyes as well, just not when she is around me. Yet, all I can say for certain is that I want my eyes to behold others in the manner that Bonnie's behold me. In her presence, I feel seen.

The Bonnies in our lives exemplify the power of presence for us. We can see both the light of their spirit shining through and the reflection of our own, because they have cultivated the habit of polishing the mirror of their awareness. They have developed ways to pause and periodically examine their thoughts and inner preoccupations. They have cultivated the habit of intentionally devoting time to clearing and cleaning the screen of their consciousness. Doing so takes time and commitment.

Perhaps that is why more of us don't do so. Time is of the essence. We prefer to gas and go through life. I know this all too well, because when it comes to driving I never take the time to stop and polish my windshield.

I tend to overrely on my windshield wipers, along with the rain or snow, to clear whatever residue accrues. When that fails, I sparingly use the cleaning solution in my vehicle's reservoir. I can spray, spray, swish, swish, and continue on my merry way without ever having to reduce my speed. It's wildly efficient, yet not incredibly effective. I'm confident that you would not be able to see your reflection clearly in my windshield, nor am I able to see clearly as I drive. My view is partial at best, often limited to the region within the arc swept clear by the windshield wipers.

The only time I get to see as clearly as possible is when I'm with my husband, Mark. Unlike me, he couldn't imagine filling up his car without cleaning his windshield. In the thirty years I have known him, there has never been a time when we've been at the gas station that he hasn't stopped to polish the windshield. It is a habit. And he has a ritual for doing so.

With all the messages coming at us as we drive through our days, we cannot rely on our windshield wipers to do the job. If we don't stop to refuel and take the time to carefully clean our windshields—that is, the screen of our consciousness—our capacity to see one another fully and clearly will be compromised and diminished. As a result, we may overlook the specific features of the terrain that another person brings to the interaction and instead focus on whatever has accumulated on the surface of our awareness. It may be the splat of a previous conversation whose sticky residue is hard to remove, an overidentification with what we want and need to get from this conversation, or our visceral sense of like or dislike for the person we're speaking with. This is the way the engine of our ego operates: conditioned reactions, attachments, and aversions.

Each of us needs Bonnies and Marks in our lives, those who model another way for us. They remind us to take the time on a regular basis to turn off our engines and get out our squeegees. They exemplify and embody for us the benefits of doing so.

ہ

What do you do, or who encourages you,
to polish the mirror of your awareness?

Practice

Today, imagine a mirror inside your heart. This mirror reflects your thoughts and inner preoccupations. Before you approach someone or speak with others, take a moment to pause and polish the mirror of your awareness. Begin by taking a deep breath to clear away the thoughts that have accrued from the previous events of the day. Take a second deep breath to cleanse away whatever residue you may find there from past interactions with this person. Take a third deep breath to set your intention to focus fully on this person, in this place, at this moment.

Keep It Fresh

Pause

Two Kinds of Intelligence

There are two kinds of intelligence: one acquired,
as a child in school memorizes facts and concepts
from books and what the teacher says,
collecting information from the traditional sciences
as well as from the new sciences.

With such intelligence you rise in the world.
You get ranked ahead or behind others
in regard to your competence in retaining
information. You stroll with this intelligence
in and out of fields of knowledge, getting always more
marks on your preserving tablets.

There is another kind of tablet, one
already completed and preserved inside of you.
A spring overflowing its springbox. A freshness
in the center of the chest. This other intelligence
does not turn yellow or stagnate. It's fluid,
and it doesn't move from outside to inside
through the conduits of plumbing-learning.

This second knowing is a fountainhead
from within you, moving out.
—Jellaladin Rumi

Ponder

I use nothing but the freshest ingredients, or so I proclaim
each time I prepare a meal. Both my husband and my son
know that my menu tends to rotate between five and
seven dishes and that the "freshest ingredients" tend to be
the only ones I happen to have on hand. In truth, my menu
is stale. As much as I aspire to add some variety to what I
prepare, cooking is not an activity that I find deeply engaging. I try to steer clear of recipes with more than a handful
of steps or those that require me to venture into unfamiliar parts of the grocery aisle in search of new ingredients.
My limited menu and lack of fresh ingredients resemble
many of the statements I hear people make in conversation. They tend to have five to seven key lines that they
keep repeating. Here is a sampling I heard, within the span
of an hour, at a recent family gathering:

"I haven't lived up to my potential."

"All men, no matter what their age, never get
beyond the mentality of a fourteen-year-old" (said
by a man).

"That's the way our family is; we'll never change."

We utter these statements about ourselves, others, groups
of people, or events as if they were empirically verifiable

rather than a matter of opinion or limited perception. We don't seem to believe that we or others are capable of change or recognize how much our words influence our perception of reality.

I recently spoke with a middle-aged woman who lamented about being the invisible child in her family. She proceeded to recite a litany of complaints about each of her siblings' treatment of her. As I listened, I noticed that, as she talked, she barely paused to take a breath. I wasn't sure that I would be able to get a word in edgewise. However, she finally paused to take a long sip of her wine. I had my chance and so I asked, "What if a magic genie suddenly appeared and you were given three wishes for your relationship with your family? What would you ask for?" She seemed intrigued by the question rather than irritated by it. She paused before she responded. As she began to speak, I noticed that her tone had shifted. Instead of ranting about all the things she wanted family members to stop doing (for example, stop drinking so much, stop taking her for granted, stop ignoring her), she began to describe what she hoped they *would* do (for example, live healthy lives, convey their appreciation of her, hang out with her). I was relieved to see that she didn't have a rehearsed answer to my question. Instead, I had hoped that my question would invite her to offer a real-time response, to turn her attention to *the freshness in the center of her chest*.

Although many of us may aspire to keep it fresh and use only the freshest ingredients, we often find that we tend to work with the limited ingredients we have on hand. When it comes to cooking, I am especially grateful when someone shows me how to prepare something new or a way to enhance a recipe I have been making for some time. And this is what the Sufi poet Jellaladin Rumi does for me regarding conversation. He reminds me that we all possess a second intelligence. The first kind of intelligence is acquired—based on the messages and lessons we have been told by others. The second type is discovered—in the moment, by paying attention to the *freshness in the center of our chests*.[10] On occasion, the freshest response we can offer one another is accepting responsibility for what we have said (or done) and resolving to make amends. We've all had those moments when words spring forth from our mouth and we realize, "I didn't mean to say that." At times we may ask ourselves, "That isn't true, so why did I say it?" Although it may have been true at one point, it is no longer true.

We need one another to help us keep it fresh, whether in the kitchen or in conversation. Just as the best cooks emphasize that it's important to use the freshest ingredients in any recipe, the best conversation partners do the same thing. We can ask one another questions, inviting each other to *turn to the freshness in the center of our chests* and offer real-time responses rather than rote, rehearsed, reactive ones. We can encourage one another to venture into unfamiliar parts of the aisles of our lived experience to see if there may be more nourishing ingredients to be found there.

What is one of the lines you hear yourself repeating that you would like to substitute with more nourishing ingredients?

Practice

This day, begin by focusing your attention on the *freshness in the center of your chest.* You may find it helpful to close your eyes, place your hand on your heart, and breathe deeply. As you do, you may begin to notice a vibration awakening there, *a spring overflowing its springbox.* Take your time and allow this vibration to arise. Throughout the day, periodically pause and return your attention to this *freshness in the center of your chest.* Experiment with turning your attention to this freshness as you engage in conversation.

Listen Generously

Pause

> In this culture the soul and the heart too often
> go homeless. Listening creates a holy silence.
> When you listen generously to people, they can
> hear the truth in themselves, often for the first
> time. And in the silence of listening, you can
> know yourself in everyone. Eventually you may
> be able to hear, in everyone and beyond everyone,
> the unseen singing softly to itself and to you.
> —Rachel Naomi Remen, *My Grandfather's*
> *Blessings: Stories of Strength, Refuge, and Belonging*

Ponder

Angela was feeling frustrated and bored at work. She had asked to meet with Mary, her mentor. She began by telling Mary about how she typically feels highly engaged in her work, yet at the moment she was struggling to channel her creativity. Mary then asked, "What do you love about your work?" Angela had to pause and reflect before responding, "I love being challenged and learning." Mary's question had surprised her. She had anticipated that Mary would listen and then offer her advice. Instead, Mary had invited her to listen to her core and articulate her deepest aspirations. Mary then invited Angela to think about the areas at their workplace, General Mills, where she could nourish her curiosity and her desire to learn. Angela described her interest in offering some training. Following their conversation, Mary reached out to the woman who develops the training curriculum. Shortly thereafter, Angela linked up and was invited to create a module for digital training.

Mary seems to know intuitively what organizational consultants like David Whyte emphasize. The depth and usefulness of the outer conversations we participate in depend upon our capacity to engage our inner conversations. It is often useful to have someone help us with this. Whyte observes:

> Conversation is the heart of human life and conversation is also the heart of commerce. If we take a moment to think about it, every organization must keep several different conversations vital at once. Firstly, a conversation with the unknown future gathering around their industry or their products; secondly, a conversation with their customers or the people they serve right now; and thirdly, the conversation that occurs between those who actually work together in the organization. But the depth and usefulness of *all* these outer conversations depend upon an internal conversation

that is occurring within each individual. It is very difficult to make any of those outer, abstract conversations real if the people who come in through the door every day have no real conversation with their own individuality.[11]

"Enabling discovery by listening generously," Mary reflected. "That's my purpose." Whether it's engaging with protégés or fellow employees, recruiting students on college campuses, or meeting with consumers, Mary invites those with whom she speaks to "go a layer deeper"—to have a conversation with their own individuality. She does this by asking questions that invite them to explore beneath their surface concern what is at the heart of the matter for them.

Going a layer deeper is foundational to generous listening and noticeably different than the way we typically listen. Let's face it. For most of us most of the time, listening is a means to an end rather than an end in itself. We listen in order to get our turn to talk, whether it's to give advice, advocate our position, analyze another's issues, or try to solve their problems. Generous listening provides an alternative to these conventional approaches. Oftentimes, the most generous response we can offer someone is to listen attentively without comment, interruption, or interjection.

Generous listening challenges us to go beyond the active listening so many of us have been taught. In active listening, we are instructed to paraphrase back the thoughts and feelings we hear someone expressing. Had she practiced active listening, Mary most likely would have responded, "I hear that you are not being sufficiently challenged in your work and that you are feeling frustrated." The benefit of active listening is that it offers a way for us to convey that we are in fact paying attention to what someone is saying. Yet, the practice of active listening does not necessarily help us explore what is at the heart of the matter for each of us. To do that, we need to ask one another questions that encourage us to listen deeply within to our core and identify what we most need, want, or value in the present moment. In Angela's case, she wanted to find ways to reengage with her work and her workplace. Mary's questions encouraged her to explore how to do so.

"I didn't realize how one simple conversation could have such an impact," Mary remarked after reading Angela's Facebook post later that day: "I just got excited about work again in who knows how long. Thanks, Mary, for helping me see and know that you can't ever really max out on trying to maximize an experience as long as you look hard enough and have an awesome sponsor like you ☺."

Renowned listener and beloved teacher, Douglas Steere, would not have been surprised. Steere was writing about listening long before it became the topic courant in organizational development circles. He believed that "to 'listen' another's soul into a condition of disclosure and discovery may be almost the greatest service that any human being ever performs for another."[12]

Through generous listening in even the briefest conversations, we can offer others an anchoring, calming presence in the midst of the seas they are navigating. On other more spacious occasions, we can provide a safe harbor. It's not so much the length or duration of a conversation that matters; it's all about the quality of attention and the intention we bring to it.

How do you offer a generous
listening presence to others?
What do you enjoy about
listening in this manner?
What do you find challenging
about listening in this way?

Practice

This day, be on the lookout for those to whom you can offer a generous listening presence. Listen to them attentively without comment, interruption, or interjection. If it seems helpful, *go a layer deeper* by asking a question that will invite them to listen more deeply within themselves to discover and articulate what they most need, want, or value.

Ask Heart-Awakening Questions

Pause

No other person can ever chart a course for you,
but a friend and a host who is really present can
at times firm up what you in your own deepest
heart of hearts have already felt drawing at you.

—Douglas Steere, *On Being Present Where You Are*

Ponder

"Have you every told your story before?"

"No."

"Why not?"

"No one ever asked."

Dave Isay wanted to change that. In 2003, he set up a recording booth in Grand Central Station and launched the StoryCorps Project. Isay had learned, through his work as a documentary radio producer, that a microphone gives people permission to ask questions of others that they normally wouldn't ask. Since then, close to fifty thousand people have been asked by a friend or family member to share their stories in one of the StoryCorps recording booths found throughout the country. Isay reflects in his book *Ties That Bind*, "We can discover the most profound and exquisite poetry in the words and stories of the noncelebrated people around us, if we just have the courage to ask meaningful questions and the patience to listen closely to the answers."[13]

Asking meaningful questions requires courage because asking is such a countercultural activity in our tell culture, observes Edgar Schein in his recent book, *Humble Inquiry: The Gentle Art of Asking Instead of Telling*. Schein has taught and studied organizational dynamics throughout his career and observes,

> Our pragmatic, problem-solving culture values people who know things and tell others what they know. In such a culture, having to ask is perceived to be a sign of weakness or ignorance. Asking temporarily empowers the other person in the conversation and temporarily makes me vulnerable.[14]

Those with the most authority tend to tell more often than ask, and those who ask are often viewed as either naive or bothersome or both. Case in point: Just last week, a client recalled how her boss told her *not to ask* so many questions during meetings. He insisted, "It makes it seem as if you don't know what you're doing." Yet the primary benefits of asking, according to Schein, are that we generate better ideas, make fewer errors in judgment, and increase our agility.

Our tell culture is so pervasive that many of the questions we do ask are just another form of telling. Our questions reveal our assumptions, reflect our projections, and relay our agendas. In asking questions, we often have an answer already in mind. For example:

Do you really think that [x, y, or z] is a good idea?

Have you always been so overly concerned with what your boss thinks of you?

Have you thought about using this approach instead?

We tend to offer thinly veiled advice through our questions instead of seeking to better understand another's perspective.

The remainder of the questions we ask are generally conventional in nature. They require very little effort to ask and even less effort to answer. Conventional questions are designed to elicit information. They take on predictable forms at all stages of our lives:

How do you like school? (we ask the children we meet).

What is your major? (we ask the students we meet).

What do you do for a living? (we ask the adults we meet).

When I'm talking with someone whose repertoire is limited to conventional questions, I often feel like I'm a Pez dispenser (remember those wonderful candy containers?). With each subsequent question, I pop out another prefabricated Pez tablet. All the while, the energy in my container, along with my engagement in the conversation, diminishes. What would happen if we asked instead:

> What do you like most about the grade you are in?
>
> What are you enjoying learning about this semester?
>
> Where are you finding joy in your life these days?

Such questions cannot be answered automatically. They require real-time reflection. When asked, the other person may respond, "I need to think about that." Or "I've never thought about that before." You know you've asked a really good question when you hear that response. And that is the second part of Dave Isay's wisdom: Not only do we need to have the courage to ask meaningful questions, but we also need to have the patience to listen closely for the answers.

Asking good questions requires courage, patience, and, as Edgar Schein underscores, skill and art. He defines *humble inquiry* as "the skill and the art of drawing someone out, of asking questions to which you do not already know the answer, of building a relationship based on curiosity and interest in the other person."[15]

I've found the following guidelines especially helpful in developing the skill and practicing the art of asking heart-awakening questions:

- If you think you already know how the other person will respond, try to come up with a different question.

- Begin your question with words and phrases like these: *how, what, where, when, in what ways ...* or *tell me more about ...* Open-ended questions tend to evoke more robust responses because they cannot typically be answered *yes, no,* or in a few words.

- Pay attention to key words and phrases that seem to have particular energy and meaning for those with whom you are speaking and incorporate their language into your question. For example, What are you getting *jazzed* about these days? What *hit you at your core* in that meeting? Tell me more about what *floats your boat* in this design.

- Maintain awareness of a person's nonverbal responses and incorporate your observations into your questions. For example, I notice how your eyes lit up when you talked about yesterday's presentation. What was the highlight of that presentation for you?

- Go beyond the first response. Encourage others to keep noticing and naming what's at the core, the heart of the matter for them. For example, Tell me more about why that is important to you.

- Continue to listen patiently as our deepest truths are often difficult to put into words quickly and continue to emerge over time.

What is a question you would most
like to be asked and by whom?

Practice

This day, in each of the conversations you participate in, try to ask at least one heart-awakening question. As much as possible, tailor your question to the unique aspects of the person—being attentive to his or her manner of speaking, preferred phrases, and expressions.

Speak about Growth and Possibility

Pause

In most of psychology, researchers describe what is. Often they do this with great acumen and creativity. But *knowing what is and knowing what can be are not the same thing.* My interest, for as long as I can remember, is in what can be, and in learning what subtle changes might make that happen. My research has shown how using a different word, offering a small choice, or making a subtle change in the physical environment can improve our health and well-being. Small changes can make large differences, so we should open ourselves to the impossible and embrace a psychology of possibility.

—Ellen Langer, *Counter-Clockwise:*
Mindful Health and the Power of Possibility

Ponder

I can still hear their voices and see their faces. The first I'll call Jack, my designated mentor at a for-profit educational consulting firm where I interned for a semester while I was in graduate school. As such, I thought it might be a good idea to run by him the interview questions I had designed for a study exploring the impact of organizational change on personal well-being. As I read him the proposed questions, he guffawed, "You don't honestly think that middle-aged men will answer your questions, do you?" The second I'll call Ted, one of the members of a nonprofit's leadership team that I was hired to coach. When he heard that I had been invited to cofacilitate a discussion with their founder, he asked, "You don't honestly think that he will share the stage with you, do you?" The third I'll call Dale, a corporate leader with a commitment to teambuilding, whom I met as I was preparing to launch the Journey Conversations Project (which I direct). After briefly looking at the materials I had generated for the project website, he glibly asked, "You don't honestly think you can make a living at this, do you?"

In all three cases, my response was: Yes, I honestly think *they would, he would,* and *I could.* I acknowledge that there may have been a grain of truth in what each of them had to say. Nonetheless, my most charitable interpretation of their reactions is that each of them was trying to protect me from unnecessary disappointment. My least charitable interpretation is that all three of them were projecting their own fears onto me. Whether their responses stemmed from protection or projection, they in no way stemmed from a mind-set of growth and possibility. Instead, their comments seemed to reflect a fixed mind-set about what others would do and what I was capable of doing.

In her book *Mindset: The New Psychology of Success*, psychologist Carol Dweck draws on her extensive research findings on fixed versus growth mind-sets. Those with a fixed mind-set believe their basic qualities, such as intelligence and talent, are simply fixed traits. As a result, they focus their energy on proving how intelligent or talented they are (or concluding that they have little to none), rather than developing their intelligence or talents. Dweck and other psychologists have found that the belief in fixed ability is completely wrong. Abilities of all kinds are profoundly malleable. Those with a growth mind-set believe that their most basic abilities can be developed through dedication and hard work—that our brains and talent are just the starting point. Dweck emphasizes that one of the best ways we can cultivate a growth mind-set is by focusing our conversations with one another on effort and learning. Dweck encourages us to ask one another questions like these:

> What did you learn today?
>
> What mistake did you make that taught you something?
>
> What did you try hard at today?[16]

As I reflect back on my conversations with Jack, Ted, and Dale, and other conversations like those, I know that it would have made all the difference had they asked:

> What do you hope to learn from your research?
>
> What would you like to contribute through your cofacilitation?
>
> What difference do you hope to make through the work of this project?

Instead of offering me their assessment of my situation, I wish they had inquired about what I hoped to learn, accomplish, and change through my efforts.

Another contemporary psychologist whose work focuses on understanding mind-sets and increasing our capacity to become more mindful is Ellen Langer. She observes:

Too many of us believe the world is to be discovered, rather than a product of our own construction and thus to be invented. We often respond as if we and/or the world around us are fixed, even when we agree in theory that we are not…. There are many cynics out there who are entrenched in their beliefs and hold dear their view of the world as fixed and predictable. There are also people who, while not cynical, are still mindlessly accepting of these views. A new approach to psychology and to our lives is needed because the naysayers—those who demand empirical evidence—are winning. It is they who have determined what's possible and what's achievable, to our collective detriment. If we suggest a possibility that seems far afield from what is currently known, the burden of proof is on us. Yet rather than ask "How could that be?" it makes just as much sense to ask "Why couldn't it be so?"[17]

Why couldn't it be so? I want to dwell in possibility rather than delimit possibility. As a parent, partner, advisor, teacher, and friend, I know I too have been guilty of mindlessly speaking words that delimit others' possibilities and deflate their spirits. In an effort to speak more mindfully, with greater openness and possibility, I try to remember to pause and THINK before I speak. If time permits, I try to reflect upon all the following questions before I do:

T—Is it true?

H—Is it helpful?

I—Is it inspiring?

N—Is it necessary?

K—Is it kind?

✢

Who has invited you to reflect upon what you hope to learn and accomplish through your efforts? How have you responded?

Practice

This day, take a moment to pause and THINK before you respond in conversation. Is what I am about to say true? Is it helpful? Is it inspiring? Is it necessary? Is it kind? If it doesn't meet all five criteria, then take time to reTHINK what you are about to say.

Part Three

Cultivating Engaging Communities

Learn from Everyone

Pause

> It was for me the start of a lesson that I never stop
> having to learn: to pay attention to the things I'll
> probably never need to know, to listen carefully
> to the people who look as if they have nothing to
> teach me, to see school as something that goes
> on everywhere, all the time, not just in librar-
> ies but in parking lots, in airports, in trees.
> —Ann Patchett, *What Now?*

Ponder

On weekends, I expect to find special events taking
place at the parkways that surround the Mississippi
River here in downtown Minneapolis. One of the most
common places for crowds to gather is around the
band-shell stage at Hennepin Bluffs Park on historic
Main Street. I like walking among them and prefer to
keep moving rather than congregating among the large
crowds. On a recent weekend walk in that park, I had
no intention of slowing down until I saw someone who
captivated my attention: an elderly man dressed in a
costume. As I looked more closely at the small sign next

to him, I saw that it read "the Baron of Bubble"! The baron was holding the biggest bubble wand I had ever seen or will probably ever see again. There was a young couple on bikes in front of me and they appeared to be as surprised at the sight of him as I was. Perhaps that was because he wasn't standing on the band-shell stage; he stationed himself right alongside the beaten path. At his side was a large bucket of bubble-making solution. He wasn't making a loud ruckus and calling attention to himself or his product by proclaiming, "Come make your bubbles—the biggest bubbles ever." He wasn't selling his services or expecting a donation (I saw no container for loose change or dollar bills). Instead, he avidly watched all who approached and looked into their eyes to see whether or not they were drawn to creating bubbles.

A young boy had just returned a bubble wand to the bucket. The baron asked the woman on the bike if she'd like to try it. She initially declined, and then he turned to me. He knew what my answer would be. "I have to try it!" I exclaimed. I then encouraged her to do the same. I suggested that she give it a go first. The baron demonstrated how to open the band on the wand as the air filled it and how to close the band once a bubble had reached ample size. She then dipped the wand into the bubble solution. Although her first try did not yield any bubbles, her second attempt did. I was transfixed by her creation and so was she. Then it was my turn.

I dunked the wand in the secret bubble sauce and opened the band. A bubble formed and filled and ascended ever so effortlessly. And my amusement rose in tandem with that bubble. When I closed the band to seal the bubble shut, I felt such a delight-filled sense of accomplishment. The baron seemed equally delighted. I thanked the baron, returned to the path, and made my way home. As I did, I walked with a different cadence.

The following day, I couldn't shake the experience with the baron of bubble. I don't want to exaggerate it to the point of seeming silly, yet for whatever reason I had paid attention to a thing I'll probably never need to know (creating large bubbles); listened carefully to people who look as if they have nothing to teach me (an old man dressed in a baron costume); and seen school "as something that goes on everywhere, all the time, not just in libraries but in parking lots, in airports, in trees" (and in my neighborhood park).[1] And here's what I had learned as a result: The baron met people on the path they were on. He didn't seem to have any agenda beyond engaging those who were interested in learning about an activity he found delightful. He wanted to share his love of bubbles with others. His gift was freely offered with no expectation of anything in return. He extended an invitation, offered some brief instructions, and then entrusted participants to experiment with the process. As I reflected further, I understood why I was so riveted: he embodied the essence of what the very best teachers and leaders so often do.

The past couple of weekends, I hold out hope that I may once again see the baron when I walk through that park. I sometimes wonder whether he actually existed. In the meantime, I'm on the lookout, eager to learn something from all those I encounter, whether they're dressed in costumes or not.

Who have you encountered who initially looked
as if they had nothing to teach you?
Think of one from whom you ended up
learning a lot. Who was the person?
How did you meet each other?
What did you learn from him or her?

Practice

This day, begin by pausing and reflecting upon all those people you are scheduled to meet. As various people come to mind, set your intention to be curious about what you can learn from them. Throughout the day, try to notice all those who cross your path, familiar and unfamiliar. Keep in mind a simple question: What can I learn from you? At the close of the day, reflect upon everyone you met today, both planned and unplanned, and call to mind one person in particular from whom you learned something unexpected.

Act on
What Matters

Pause

This culture, and we as members of it, have yielded
too easily to what is doable and practical and popu-
lar. In the process we have sacrificed the pursuit
of what is in our hearts. We find ourselves giving
in to our doubts, and settling for what we know
how to do, or can soon learn how to do, instead of
pursuing what most matters to us and living with
the adventure and anxiety that this requires.

—Peter Block, *The Answer to How Is Yes:
Acting on What Matters*

Ponder

I immediately contacted the chair of the Fetzer
Institute's board, Rob Lehman, once I learned that
the institute's model of community and governance
is one of deep engagement. I was eager to find out
more about how Fetzer officials understood and practiced deep engagement as an organization. Like leaders of any philanthropic foundation, they get numerous

unsolicited requests. So I was unsure whether or not I would receive a response to my inquiry. Perhaps a no more telling indication of their commitment to deep engagement was that not only did I receive an enthusiastic response directly from Rob, but I also received it within a week. Moreover, he invited three other members of the Fetzer community to join us for our initial conversation.

As we began our conversation, Rob reflected upon how important the notion of a community of freedom was to their founder, John Earl Fetzer. Fetzer aspired to create a foundation that would carry out its mission for three hundred to five hundred years and wondered what kind of organization might promote that kind of continuity over time. The Fetzer Institute community came to embody his vision, as articulated in this way:

> A community of freedom is a living network of authentic relationships among people who are engaged in a journey of discovering and living out their unique callings, sharing their gifts and the quest for freedom and spirit. Living in a community of freedom also calls on members to embrace the responsibility of freedom and to strive to live and speak with authenticity, compassion, and respect for diversity.[2]

From this foundational commitment to cultivating a community of freedom the institute's deep engagement model of community subsequently emerged. The life-blood of deep engagement for the institute is found in communication, dialogue, and relationships that are "deeply engaged" in three fundamental senses:

- Engaged individuals who hold a commitment to deepening their own interior life, their spiritual life, and have a willingness to promote that same effort collectively.
- An engaged community whose members are committed to cultivating and practicing the skills for deep listening and deep sharing.
- Engaged leaders who are committed to shared leadership and to a participatory process of tackling issues and determining directions.

As Fetzer's current president Bob Boisture points out: "Initially, our focus on deep engagement began with the board and senior staff. We've broadened that substantially over the last year to really underscore that it's got to be the whole community. And so we've begun devoting three hours each Wednesday morning from nine to noon to bring our entire staff of sixty-five together for a Community of Freedom gathering. These gatherings are designed to deepen our individual and collective spiritual grounding as well as develop dialogue skills."[3]

As a person who has worked in program evaluation, I wanted to know more about the impact of these gatherings (which had begun six months earlier). Two of the

staff members—Deborah Yeager and Kathy Cavanaugh—told me about three of the signs of success they
have witnessed to date: they are hearing much less concern from other staff about giving up a half day each
week; the original group of planners has rotated and
now includes more members taking on a direct role
in helping create these gatherings; and they are seeing
people from all departments taking on a leadership role.
For instance, during a recent gathering that focused on
the topic of vocation, a groundskeeper read a poem and
someone from the kitchen staff led a meditation.

As encouraging as that all sounded, what I also
wanted to ask was this: Are they noticing a deepening engagement among community members outside
of these Wednesday morning gatherings? Yes, and …
they'd like to see even more. It is incumbent upon the
senior staff members to model deep engagement as well
as encourage their team members to practice it. This
model requires individuals who possess immense self-
awareness, maturity of spirit, discernment, and judgment, and leaders who hold themselves, their staffs,
and the board accountable.

I was struck by their candor in pointing out the
dangers inherent in implementing this approach—the
shadow side of such a lofty, ambitious model. They have
named one manifestation of shadow they've encountered a "culture of politeness"—that is, taking the idea
of respectful dialogue and misinterpreting it as just

having to be nice to each other. At a recent Wednesday morning gathering, they discussed that even the phrase *culture of politeness* was too polite. Their growing collective awareness is that it's more accurately described as a culture of fear and aversion because "we're afraid that whatever portion of the community we're interacting with in a particular context may not live up to our values. As a result, we don't lean into problems. We avoid them."

Deep engagement as a model for community and governance is a demanding vision that cannot be legislated or enforced, only nurtured and sustained. Enacting such a vision will always be a work in progress. There is a tension inherent in building a relationship-centered community while at the same time building an organization that can advance its mission in a creative, disciplined, and efficient manner.

My friends at Fetzer are often asked, "With such high aspirations, how do you walk your talk?" Their response: "We walk our talk by falling down and getting up, or better by falling down and helping each other get up. We can only do this with the help of each other. A deeply engaged organization is not about perfection; it is about wholeness—about love and forgiveness." How fitting that an organization whose mission is fostering awareness of the power of love and forgiveness in the emerging global community embraces Gandhi's words, "being the change they wish to see in the world."

As I listened to all four members of the Fetzer community speak of their convictions and commitments, I found my admiration growing. I thought of Peter Block's words, found in this chapter's opening epigraph, that rather than *settling for what they know how to do, or can soon learn how to do*, they are *pursuing what most matters to them and living with the adventure and anxiety that this requires*.[4] Moreover, I especially applaud their effort to keep moving the bar deeper rather than settling for superficial or limited expressions of the engagement they so seek to embody.

⌁

> What action would you undertake if you
> weren't concerned about how to do it?

Practice

This day, undertake an activity that reflects what most matters to you. It may be signing up for a class, beginning to read a new book, sharing a cup of coffee with a colleague, or reconnecting with someone with whom you've been out of touch. It need not be grand, and it need not be long term. What's important is that you initiate a small step in pursuit of what matters most to you at this moment.

Fan the Flame

Pause

Sometimes our light goes out but is blown into flame
by another human being. Each of us owes deepest
thanks to those who have rekindled this light.
> —Albert Schweitzer

The light shed by any good relationship
illuminates all relationships.
> —Anne Morrow Lindbergh, *Gift from the Sea*

Ponder

Did you know that research has found that most of us
are surprisingly unaware of which experiences make
us happy and which do not? That is why psychologist
Sonja Lyubomirsky encourages people to keep a journal documenting which daily experiences—people,
events, situations, or activities—generate positive emotions for them. In her book, *The Myths of Happiness: What
Should Make You Happy But Doesn't, What Shouldn't Make
You Happy But Does*, she reports that the key to happiness and health is the frequency of experiencing ordinary bursts of happiness rather than the intensity of the

elation. Some of the most commonly overlooked experiences of happiness are those we receive through our everyday interactions.

If I were to keep a journal of the people who bring happiness to my life, you would find Mohamed frequently mentioned. If you were to visit our condominium building, I suspect you would mention him as well. For the past thirteen years, Mohamed has been bringing happiness to our guests and those of us who reside here. He is a leader who models the way for others—ever alert and ever ready to offer assistance to those who walk through the door or up to his desk. He exemplifies a way of being that I aspire to attain. I most often see him talking with or assisting another resident. On a rare occasion, I see him sitting quietly at his desk. While there, he doesn't occupy himself with reading, watching television, or working on the computer. Instead, he seems to be focusing on the present moment, ever vigilant for whatever need might arise in it. In many cases, it's by deliberately getting up from his chair, personally opening the door, and greeting us by name (as opposed to simply pushing the button next to his chair). When he speaks, he looks directly into a person's eyes and asks, "How are you doing today?" He then waits and listens to the response. I marvel at how he remembers details about our lives without being nosy or intrusive. What makes this level of attentiveness and care all the more amazing to me is that I know he works a second job in the evening. In truth, I don't know how he does it. Yet I do know that interacting with Mohamed consistently uplifts me. Although our interactions are often brief and at times consist of merely a greeting, they are frequent and dependably pleasant—so much so that I often make it a point to walk by the front desk because of the happiness speaking with him brings me.

And then there are those whose desks I would rather avoid because of the distress speaking with them brings me. Whether it's a "problem person" in the workplace or a difficult member of our family, it is tempting to avoid those people who tend to bring us down. Yet, organizational development consultant and author Gervase Bushe offers us another way: tracking and fanning.[5]

Tracking is a state of mind that begins with the assumption that whatever we would like to see more of in others already exists, even if in small amounts. Perhaps the difficult people in my life possess thoughtfulness, care, and concern, as Mohamed does, and I just need to look deeper to see it. Through tracking, we focus our attention on constantly looking for more of the characteristics and behaviors we want to see. Once we see one, we then fan it. Fanning is any action that amplifies, encourages, and affirms the pleasant characteristics we notice.

Tracking and fanning take effort on our part. While it may sound similar to behavioral reinforcement, it demands more from us than simply reinforcing desired behaviors. It requires a change of consciousness in us. We must believe, even in the face of contradictory evidence, that another person does possess desirable characteristics. Such characteristics just need to be recognized to be rekindled.

I used to think that happiness stemmed from the great, extraordinary moments of my life. As Lyubomirsky and other psychologists who study happiness are finding, we tend to overestimate how blissful we will feel after a big gain or how dejected we will feel after a big loss. We also underestimate how many other events will intervene to temper our pleasure or mitigate our pain. Each of us has the potential to mitigate others' pain and offer bursts of happiness through our daily interactions. Where our attention goes, grows. The more we pay attention to people who uplift us and what they do to make us feel good, the more we can replicate those behaviors in more of our relationships. The more we can look for examples of the good we seek in others, the more likely we will be to find them.

∽

Which people in your life make you consistently
feel uplifted when you're in their presence?
What do they do that generates
positive emotions for you?

Practice

This day, select a person you find difficult to be around. Rather than paying attention to the behaviors you don't like in another person, focus on trying to find something that is admirable and worthy of affirmation. It may be his concern for his children or her creative choice of words in a comment made at a recent meeting. Your mission is to track and find a characteristic or a behavior to appreciate and then to fan it by conveying an affirmation to him or her about it.

Scan for Joy

Pause

The Winter of Listening
Inside everyone
is a great shout of joy
waiting to be born.

Even with summer
so far off
I feel it grown in me
now and ready
to arrive in the world.

All those years
listening to those
who had
nothing to say.

All those years
forgetting
how everything
has its own voice
to make
itself heard.

All those years
forgetting
how easily
you can belong
to everything
simply by listening.

And the slow
difficulty
of remembering
how everything
is born from
an opposite
and miraculous
otherness.

Silence and winter
has led me to that
otherness.

So let this winter
of listening
be enough
for the new life
I must call my own.

—David Whyte, *The House of Belonging*

Ponder

It was the winter of 2010. The previous fall, I had been
selected to design and facilitate a strategic visioning

process for Family Matters, a community nonprofit based in Chicago. During our initial consultation, members of the strategic planning committee stressed how important it was for us to fully engage all stakeholders in the visioning process—parents, program alums, community, staff, and board members.

Every meeting creates an occasion to push the Refresh button on our way to engage with one another. The manner in which a meeting begins often sets the tone for the remainder. I knew that if we began our visioning meeting with the invitation to "tell us a bit about yourself. How long have you worked for or served on the board for Family Matters?" it would be business as usual. Conventional introductions tend to elicit rote, rehearsed responses. What we needed was a way of introducing ourselves to one another that would yield deeply engaged responses. What we needed was a catalyst. We needed to pose a question that would encourage both reflection and risk-taking, as well as offer a potential reward. The reflection: an invitation for all participants to listen to their core. The risk: to disclose and speak from a deeper level. The reward: participants might discover something new about themselves and one another.

In preparation, I returned to some of my favorite poems. When I got to the phrase *inside everyone is a great shout of joy waiting to be born*, in David Whyte's "The Winter of Listening," I felt as if the eagle had landed. I would invite participants to introduce themselves by describing one *shout of joy* they had experienced at Family Matters.

The next day, I tested out my opening question with my aunt, one of the wisdom figures in my life. I emailed her the poem and the opening question. She called me shortly thereafter, "Oh honey, it is February and the days are very gray, we are in the midst of two wars, and our economy is in shambles. I can't imagine that anyone will be able to find anything joyful to shout about." I listened and discerned. I recognized she was trying to protect me from an absolute bust-up at the beginning of an important meeting, and I appreciated her concern. Nonetheless, something within me persisted. I just knew that I had to pose this question. It was a risk I had to take. In so doing, I hoped that my willingness to take a risk and be vulnerable would encourage others to do the same.

You get from a group what you give to a group. This is one of the lessons I am learning from my work as a consultant. If you offer a question that invites participants to focus on what isn't working, they'll happily cooperate and speak on and on about all the seemingly intractable problems there are to solve. Conversely, if you invite participants to describe an aspiration or recall a time when things were working well, they'll do their best to come up with one.

And so, a week later, I stood in front of a group of more than thirty stakeholders who were willing to devote a day and a half of their weekend to cocreating a vision for Family Matters. I began by reading the excerpt from the poem "The Winter of Listening." I then invited them to share a shout of joy. I went first to model the way—in terms of tone and timing. I don't recall the shout of joy I spoke about that afternoon. I do recall that I told them the story of my aunt's concern about beginning our meeting with this question. And then I sat on the edge of the table and waited for their responses. A palpable pause followed. The connection between shouts of joy and strategic visioning didn't connect immediately. However, as each person spoke about a shout of joy that stirred within him or her (and most had a hard time limiting themselves to just one) the group began to see what they were cocreating together—a symphony of joy. Although the shared introductions lasted no more than forty-five minutes, there was a timeless quality to the exchange. What I remember most about that afternoon was how the energy in the room began to shift. Whatever initial tension there was, and there is always tension when a group first comes together, there seemed to be a force that began to embrace and uplift us. By the time we had heard from everyone, we had arrived at a new place together. I lost track of who was who—board member, staff member, attorney, accountant, parent, or past participant.

I take great joy in reporting that following the planning session, Family Matters began to infuse "shouts of joy" into their culture. If you were to visit Family Matters today, you would find that both board and staff meetings begin with shouts of joy. The teen girls begin their meetings by huddling together and offering one another "complimentary whispers": what they appreciate in each other. On the Family Matters' Twitter page and website, you will also find "shouts of joy" proclaiming the impact of their work.

Since that meeting, I too have continued to infuse "shouts of joy" into my work. I invite participants in the groups I facilitate to listen within for a shout of joy yearning to be expressed. In so doing, I also acknowledge that at one level, my aunt was right. It is difficult to find joy in the midst of bleak and challenging conditions. Her sentiment echoes the empirical findings of many organizational psychologists who remind us of our predilection for noticing what is negative. Most of us are accustomed to focusing on our problems, analyzing them, and seeking solutions. In turn, we ask one another problem-focused questions: "What's broken, and how do we fix it?" We believe that change will result by addressing what's not working.

Best-selling authors Chip and Dan Heath explore this phenomenon in *Switch: How to Change Things When Change Is Hard*. They report that big problems are rarely solved with big solutions. They have found that big problems are most often solved by a sequence of small solutions implemented over time. These small solutions

stem from a capacity to identify the bright spots—
efforts worth emulating. To make a switch and imple-
ment change, they encourage us to notice and name
what's working, and to figure out how we can do more
of it.

Our questions are tools. Our questions have conse-
quences. Really good questions have the potential to
illuminate uncharted or rarely explored terrain. Questions extend an invitation: to push the Refresh button and use our collective search engines to scan for a
response. Because there are a whole lot of files each of
us needs to process, we have to encourage one another
to be patient and wait with anticipation for a bright spot
of joy to emerge.

⚭

What is a shout of joy that is yearning
to be expressed from within you?

Practice

Today, as you move through your daily activities, notice
which persons, places, or things connect you to a shout of
joy within.

Hold the Tension

Pause

Portrait of the Heart in Darkness

There is a place beyond
light's steady breath
where all that is possible
is to hold
the impossible.

A mother with wild eyes
and empty breasts
sits silently
on sun-baked
Saharan earth.

A father hears words
he has been dreading,
and fights tears
and empty pockets
on the grimy bus ride home.

A child watches her brother
pale against white sheets,
laced with tubes

and machines,
and asks why?

There is a place
where all that is possible
is to hold the impossible.

Here, life asks only
that we place one foot
in front of the other,
that we make the bed,
that we clean the dishes.

Here, life demands
witness, demands
that we turn
towards the darkness
of the heart, demands
that we breathe
in unison
with the impossible.

Only then we may create
that place where Mystery
may blow gently
on the embers
of barely breathing coals.
        —Jennifer (Jinks) Hoffmann

Ponder

It centers me to stand at the middle of the Third Avenue Bridge in downtown Minneapolis and look down from the rail at the surging water. From there, I can see, hear, and feel the energy of the Mississippi River as it feeds into the river's largest natural waterfall. In 1680, Father Louis Hennepin beheld these falls for the first time. He named them the *Chutes de Saint-Antoine* (the Falls of Saint Anthony) after his patron saint, Anthony of Padua, a thirteenth-century Portuguese Catholic priest. It is to Saint Anthony that many pray when they need help finding lost articles or are themselves feeling lost. Perhaps that is why I find the sound of these falls so centering and grounding.

One late-spring afternoon my son, Ryan, called into my home office, "Mom, there's a bunch of police cars on the bridge." He walked out to our balcony, and I followed right after him. From there, we can see the entire span of the Third Avenue Bridge, a major passageway between our neighborhood and downtown. Typically, on a weekday afternoon during rush hour, the bridge is filled with vehicles heading north out of the city. On this day, the only vehicles in sight were police cars and other rescue vehicles blocking off traffic at each end of the bridge. In the center of the bridge, six police officers formed a semicircle right around the exact spot where I like to stand. As I looked more closely, I detected a figure there. He was standing on the outside of the rail.

I said to Ryan, "Can you see that man there? I think he's going to jump." I paused and added, "We need to practice *tonglen*. Have I told you about *tonglen*?" I then spoke about how I try to remember to practice *tonglen* whenever I'm in situations where the only thing I can do to help is to breathe.

Tonglen is the practice of *sending and taking* (based on the Tibetan word from which it derives its meaning). As spiritual teacher Susan Stabile describes in *Growing in Love and Wisdom: Tibetan Buddhist Sources for Christian Meditation*, through this practice one breathes out and *sends* love, compassion, and healing to those who are suffering; one then breathes in and *takes* on their suffering for the sake of their healing. It doesn't matter whether it's one or more persons you can literally see, as it was for my son and me, or masses of people who aren't physically present. The practice is the same. Breathe out love, comfort, and compassion; breathe in the tension, the confusion, and the difficulty.

On that particular May afternoon, my son and I felt as if we, too, were "first responders" along with all those police officers who surrounded the man on the bridge. It was as if Ryan and I (and the other bystanders looking from the sidewalk below) were completing the circle. As we watched and waited, I lost track of time. I'm not sure if it was five or fifteen minutes. Yet eventually we saw one of the man's legs and then the other return to the inside rail of the bridge. A police officer and a person in plain clothing gradually moved closer to him. Shortly thereafter, the man fell to the ground and after another few minutes, he was accompanied to a police car. While Ryan and I might have then returned to our respective activities, we didn't move until all the police officers and all the vehicles had departed from the bridge. We watched as the police car carrying the man headed south. Although it was soon enveloped in the city, the image of his figure standing on the bridge remained.

I had never imagined I would witness such a sight, and certainly not in my own backyard at my cherished spot. I will never know who that man was or whether our *tonglen* helped change his mind. But that's not the point. The real value of *tonglen* is not what it does or does not do for the object (in this case, the man on the bridge).[6] While we may never know whether our intentional breathing is of benefit to others, we can be assured that it does have a benefit for us. Practicing *tonglen* offers us a way to cherish others. It increases our compassion and diminishes the separation between our pain and others' pain. It cultivates our capacity to respond—that is, to stand in our center and hold the tensions in our hearts—rather than take flight, fight, or freeze in reaction to them.

❧

At this moment in time, whose suffering
fills your heart with concern?

Practice

Today, as you read the paper, see an accident on the side of the road, or witness anyone in distress, breathe out and send them your love, care, and compassion; breathe in and take in their suffering.

Mine the Meaning

Pause

> When we think that something is going to bring
> us pleasure, we don't know what's really going to
> happen. When we think something is going to give
> us misery, we don't know. Letting there be room
> for not knowing is the most important thing of
> all. We try to do what we think is going to help.
> But we don't know. We never know if we're going
> to fall flat or sit up tall. When there's a big disap-
> pointment, we don't know if that's the end of the
> story. It may be just the beginning of a great adven-
> ture…. Life is like that. We call something bad;
> we call it good. But really we just don't know.
>
> —Pema Chödrön, *When Things Fall Apart:*
> *Heart Advice for Difficult Times*

Listening is not about technique or paraphrasing
but about aesthetics…. Listening is the discipline
and art of capturing the complexity of history in
the simplicity of deep intuition. It is attending
to a sharp sense of what things mean…. Listening requires the discipline of very few words and

enormous patience to penetrate the great clouds of
ambiguity while living in them. People talk at and
then around things, and they go around and around
again. So many things are said and then repeated ...
Anger, bitterness, regret, sadness, loss, and misun-
derstanding are all mixed in a bundle of messages
made up of words and images, spoken and unspoken. In the midst of that very human mess, listening
is the art of connecting and finding the essence.

—John Paul Lederach, *The Moral Imagination:
The Art and Soul of Building Peace*

Ponder

I think of the following story often, especially whenever
I hear bad news (or what seems to be bad news):

An old man owned a horse. The horse ran away. Trying
to console him, his friends said, "We're so sorry about
your horse. What a misfortune." The man responded,
"Bad news, good news—who knows?"

A few days later the horse returned home, leading
a herd of wild horses. Again the friends came running.
Filled with jubilation, they cried, "How wonderful!"
But the old man responded, "Good news, bad news—
who knows?"

Then the next day, when the farmer's son was trying to ride one of the new horses, the young man was
thrown to the ground and broke both legs. The friends

gasped. The old man stood still and responded, "Bad news, good news—who knows?"

And a short time later when the village went to war and all the young men were drafted to fight, the farmer's son was given a deferment because of his two broken legs. Good news, bad news—who knows?[7]

We don't know, but we so want to know, don't we? We don't have to look very far or for very long to find someone smack dab in the midst of trying to make sense out of bad news. If we ourselves are suffering, we lament: What am I supposed to do now? If it's someone we care about, we wonder: What should I say? How can I best respond?

"The cartilage in your left knee is gone," the surgeon told my friend Tawanna. "Bone is grinding bone. Our only option is to replace the joint." He explained that the procedure would take three months of preparation (a battery of physicals, weight loss, preoperative medications, and the reorganization of her third floor condo to accommodate a walker and a cane). The recovery process would be anything but passive. The surgeon told her that he hoped the prospect of regaining her mobility, at age forty-nine, would be a sufficient incentive for her to commit to healing. He wrapped up their appointment by emphasizing that if all went as planned, she'd be dancing by December. Deep in her bones (those old and those soon-to-be new), she believed him.

Rather than resort to a rash assessment of her situation, Tawanna responded as the old man in the story does: *Bad news, good news—who knows?* Through the seemingly bad news of her pending surgery and her very real need to prepare for it, she began an intentional process of clearing and cleansing, releasing and reconnecting, letting go and reclaiming life. She spent months ridding her home of items that, though beautiful, no longer served or inspired her. Although these items had once offered comfort, now they only brought clutter. She repainted her walls, covering vibrant oranges and deep burgundies (hues that had once moved her) with soft copper, muted gray, and rich brown—colors that calm her spirit. She cleared out bundles and boxes of yellowing cards and dog-eared letters, correspondences that spanned three decades and two continents. She shredded them, one by one, and proclaimed, "I said good-bye to the girl and the young woman that had once been to make space for the woman that I was and had yet to become."

In a recent conversation, she told me: "Unbeknownst to my surgeon, the diagnosis went well beyond the limp that was the result of my degenerative knee. I have been limping through my life for a while, and I need to reclaim much more than my mobility. I want to be dancing by December."

Each of us has periods when either we, or those we are called to lead, are limping through life. We get worn down living and working in situations that are often filled with too much seemingly bad news and too little seemingly good news. Yet, as Pema Chödrön and the story of the old man underscore, *We call something bad; we call it good. But really we just don't know.*[8] Is there anything we can we do to cultivate clarity in the midst of such situations?

Peacebuilder John Paul Lederach offers a recommendation based on what he is learning: "Whenever I find myself in the middle of a tense conversation, working with or between groups involved in a serious conflict, and the situation seems endlessly complex, I ask myself a simple question: If you were to capture the heart of this thing in a sentence of fewer than eight words, what would you say?"[9] In his book, *The Moral Imagination: The Art and Soul of Building Peace*, he names this capacity the haiku moment; that is, to capture the complexity of an experience in a few words or a simple image.

Lederach believes that there is poetry embedded in every conversation. And that is why he doodles as he listens and asks himself:

- What does this thing they are describing look and feel like?
- What is at the heart of the matter?
- Where is this thing going?
- Where would they like it to go?
- What is getting in the way?
- What pictures are they painting with their words?
- What is missing from the pictures?[10]

Rather than taking notes, he occasionally writes down a word or phrase that pops out of a conversation. He also teaches haiku as an exercise in his peacebuilding classes as a way to help his students capture how their unique feelings, observations, knowledge, wisdom, and creative impulses connect them to their actions.

Most of us think of haiku as the type of poetry we wrote in grade school (thanks to cunning teachers who taught us about self-expression, syllable count, and poetry in a single assignment) and underestimate its immense value in our adult lives. In its most typical form, a haiku poem consists of only three lines and a total of seventeen syllables—the first line contains five syllables, the second seven, and the third five. This genre of poetry originated in Japan, and Bashō (living in the seventeenth century) was credited with making haiku a revered literary form. In a quotation attributed to him, he observed: "Your poetry issues of its own accord when you and the object have become one—when you have plunged deep enough into the object to see something like a hidden glimmering there." Both then and now, haiku poets aspire to humbly and sincerely see the true nature of things.

I believe the old man in the story was seeking those who could help him see the true nature of things. He wasn't interested in others' assessment of his situation or whether they thought things were good news or bad news for him. I think he was awaiting someone who would take the time to help him identify the ah-ness of the moment, to see a hidden glimmering there, a deeper truth yet to be revealed. I also believe that's what my friend and colleague Tawanna is seeking. She has already named it, in a mere seven words: *Deep in her bones … Dancing by December.*

What seemingly bad news or good news have you received that eventually revealed a deeper meaning?

Practice

Today, identify a situation in your life in which you are struggling to gain greater clarity. If you were to capture the heart of this situation in a sentence of fewer than eight words, what would you say? Is there a particular image that comes to mind as you doodle about this situation? If you feel so inclined, try writing a haiku that reflects both the words and the image.

Improvise Often

Pause

> There is a vitality, a life force, an energy, a quick-ening that is translated through you into action, and because there is only one of you in all of time, this expression is unique. And if you block it, it will never exist through any other medium and it will be lost. The world will not have it. It is not your business to determine how good it is nor how valuable nor how it compares with other expressions. It is your business to keep it yours clearly and directly, to keep the channel open.
>
> —Martha Graham, quoted by Agnes De Mille, *Martha: The Life and Work of Martha Graham—A Biography*

Ponder

The line *Make your partner look good* caught my eye as I glanced at my son Ryan's syllabus for an upcoming course in improvisation. I had always assumed that most actors (like most human beings) are more con-cerned with making themselves, rather than their part-ners, look good. And I began to wonder about how our everyday interactions might change if we focused more of our attention on *making one another look good*. My musing began in earnest after I heard the musician Herbie Hancock tell a story about what he had learned early on in his career from his mentor, Miles Davis. Herbie recalls one of his first performances with Miles at a concert in Europe:

> We had the audience in the palm of our hands. And right as everything was really peaking, and Miles was soloing, I played this chord, and it was completely wrong. And Miles took a breath and then played some notes, and the notes made my chord right.... Somehow, what he chose to play fit my chords to the structure of the music.... What I learned from that is that Miles didn't hear the chord as being wrong. He just heard it as something new that happened. So, he didn't judge it. I learned the importance of being nonjudgmental, taking what happens and trying to make it work … And it can lead you to other ideas, to something maybe you hadn't expressed before.[11]

Miles took a breath and then played some notes, and the notes made my chord right. Miles played some notes that *made his partner look good.* Like all those who improvise well onstage and in life, Miles Davis recognized that all we have to work with is what we have to work with in this moment. We can't control the chords that others play.

We can only control our response to them. Taking a deep breath helps us focus on what is happening within us and between us in the present moment. Breathing deeply increases the likelihood that we will play notes that bring out the best in others and ourselves.

Miles didn't hear the chord as being wrong. He just heard it as something new that happened. It's tempting to fixate on the wrong chords that our family members, customers, and coworkers have played in our previous encounters. Our minds like to keep replaying those chords in our internal conversations or featuring scenes from when those chords were played in our internal videos. As a result, our freedom to hear *the something new* is compromised. Even with people whose company we enjoy the most, we may lose sight of what is happening in the present moment if we are too attached to what we want to see happen instead. Whether onstage or in daily life, we all bring scripts, rehearsed lines, recollections of previous scenes from prior encounters with one another that often prevent us from noticing *the something new* happening within the other. That is why I often encourage clients to *act as if* they have amnesia (especially with people they find challenging). To encounter one another as strangers, those we are meeting for the first time, challenges us to focus on and respond to what is new in each other.

So, he didn't judge it. I learned the importance of being nonjudgmental, taking what happens and trying to make it work. In improv they call this practice accept and build rather than block and deny. One of the best ways to increase our capacity to accept and build is to say, "yes and" in response. Miles Davis *said yes* to the reality created by his partner, Herbie Hancock, *and* he built upon it by playing notes that made Hancock's chords right. By *saying yes*, we too can accept the reality created by our partners, even though that may put us in situations we would rather avoid. *Saying yes* doesn't mean that we agree with what another has done or said. Rather, it's maintaining a commitment to mutual exploration instead of argument. Saying "yes and" takes immense effort, lots of practice, and a willingness to be vulnerable. It's far easier to say "yes, but" or "no, that's not [possible, doable, workable]" rather than to find a way to engage with ideas or actions and build upon them. As tempting as it is to play it safe onstage and in our everyday conversations, we may never know what we are missing as a result.

And it can lead you to other ideas, to something maybe you hadn't expressed before. In addition to developing our capacity to accept and build upon others' responses, rather than block and deny them, an improvisational way of living challenges us to accept our own. All too often, we block or deny our internal responses. We don't go with our gut, speak our heart's truth, or give voice to our intuition. Instead, we say what we believe others want to hear or what we believe the situation warrants. In sum, we block or deny our deepest reality. The more we block and deny our own reality, the more likely we will do so with others. Keith Johnstone, one of the foremost teachers of the craft, observes in his book *Impro: Improvisation and the Theatre* that our fear of embarrassment and our unwillingness to be vulnerable are the primary reasons most of us don't improvise well. Rather than offering our most immediate response spontaneously in the moment, we tend to overthink and give our second or third response instead. That is why Johnstone works with his students to help them reconnect with their instincts or, as Martha Graham underscored, *to keep the channel open*. The more we do, the more we may discover newer and truer ways of expressing ourselves with one another.

The art of improvisation pushes us out of our comfort zone and patterned ways of speaking and responding. I speak from experience, because I, too, had enrolled in an improv course when I was my son's age. I lasted for only one session. Given my predilection for advance planning and composure, I resisted offering the required spontaneity and disclosure. After my one and only class, I decided I could more fully appreciate the art of improv as a viewer than as a participant. I'm reconsidering that decision. I'd really like to learn how to take more deep breaths, to concentrate more of my attention on what's happening in the here and now, to accept and build upon more and more of what others offer me, and to be on the lookout for what might emerge between us. I want to *keep the channel open*.

Who do you know who consistently works
to make others look good?
What does this person say or do
that brings out the best in others?

Practice

This day, aim to improvise often, especially in your conversations. Concentrate your attention on the present moment, try to accept whatever is happening within you and between you and build upon it (rather than block or deny it). Practice saying yes, *and* (rather than *yes, but* or *no, that's not*) and notice what emerges as a result.

Concentrate on the Relationships

Pause

Do not depend on the hope of results ... You may have to face the fact that your work will be apparently worthless and even achieve no result at all, if not perhaps results opposite to what you expect. As you get used to this idea, you start more and more to concentrate not on the results, but on the value, the rightness, the truth of the work itself.... You gradually struggle less and less for an idea and more and more for specific people.... In the end, it is the reality of personal relationship that saves everything.

—Thomas Merton, *The Hidden Ground of Love: Letters by Thomas Merton on Religious Experience and Social Concerns*

Ponder

Although he led the nation in rushing and scoring as a senior at Wake Forest in 1964, not a single team drafted him. Eventually, the Chicago Bears signed him as a free agent. His professional football career with the Bears spanned a mere four seasons. During those years, from 1966 to 1969, he rarely started and scored only four touchdowns. In 1970, he died of cancer.

From a results perspective, Brian Piccolo's work seems pretty worthless. I learned about Brian's football career from the film *Brian's Song*. I was nine years old when I saw it for the first time. Tears began to fill my eyes as I watched Piccolo say good-bye to his teammate and best friend, Gale Sayers. As the movie approached its conclusion, I was relieved to be by myself so that I could cry freely. That's exactly what I did as I watched the final scene—featuring Sayers and Piccolo on a run in the park. Ever the competitors, they are racing. As they do, the camera slowly pans in for a close-up of Brian's face. As it does, you hear the voice-over narration of their coach, George Halas: "What was most remarkable about his life was not how he died. It was how he lived. And, oh how he lived."

As a nine-year-old, viewing the movie for the first time, I remember being saddened by Brian's death and by the reality of death in general. Nonetheless, it was Gale Sayers's life that I most wanted to live. I wanted to be the star, the award winner, and the center of attention. And for those who know anything about Sayers's career, he was all that and more. I especially admired Sayers's commitment to his friendship with Brian. I was intrigued that Sayers had titled his memoir *I Am Third*. After I learned that his reason for doing so was based upon his credo, "The Lord is first, my friends are second, and I am third," that became my credo, too.

Almost thirty years passed between my first viewing of *Brian's Song* and the second. Ironically, I had a son who was now nine and his teacher had shown *Brian's Song* to their third-grade class. When I heard this, I asked her if I could borrow the movie. Given my response to the first viewing, I waited for an occasion to watch it on my own. I am glad I did. This time, the tears didn't wait for the conclusion. They persisted throughout. And at the end of the movie, they didn't stop. Since I don't tend to cry a lot, this caught my attention. What were all these tears about?

I didn't find it surprising that, as a thirty-nine-year-old, watching the same movie for the second time, I noticed entirely different things. What I did find surprising was noting what those differences were. Rather than being riveted by Gayle Sayers's life, as I had been at nine, I was now enamored of Brian's—his tenacity, resilience, and joyful spirit. How did he do it? Even though he spent most of his time on the bench, he kept on keeping on, he gave the game and his team all he had to give, and he did whatever he could whenever he could to bring joy to others. I also marveled at Brian's capacity to maintain such a fierce commitment to both his work and his friendship with Sayers—his teammate who set records while Brian watched from the sidelines.

I have since learned that Piccolo had beat out two-time All-American Sayers in rushing and scoring during his senior year in college. Yet, the NFL scouts had underestimated Piccolo and believed the 5-foot-11,190-pound running back wasn't big enough or fast enough. Would his football career have been any different if he hadn't played for the Bears? We'll never know. What we do know is that he hardly ever escaped Sayers's overwhelming shadow. A rare exception was in the second half of the 1968 season. That season Sayers suffered a ruptured cartilage and two torn ligaments in his right knee, and, as a result, Piccolo got to start. In the movie, we see Sayers returning home on crutches. As he hobbles down to the basement, he finds Brian ready to greet him with a weight machine. Brian said (and I'm paraphrasing), "I'm going to get you as strong as you were before the injury, if not stronger, so that I can beat you next season."

Most of us experience a shift in perspective between nine and thirty-nine. We've spent our time on the bench watching others set records. We've initiated a lot of different actions and experienced disappointment and lack of fruition. As I watched *Brian's Song* the second time, I'm sure the unacknowledged grief of many of my failed or partially fulfilled dreams were surfacing in my consciousness. However, I know that the tears were a reflection of not only my grief; they were also a reflection of my deep admiration, my values. I just love that Brian stayed in the game. He remained deeply engaged.

Whether on the bench, or on the field, he was ready to play. He was there for his team. He wanted to give both the game and his team his all.

In the Bhagavad Gita, Lord Krishna advises a young warrior, Arjuna, on the eve of battle, *Be intent on action, not the fruits of action.*[12] Our lives are an ongoing battle. We live in a results-oriented culture, a culture that values winning and scoring lots of touchdowns. It seems far sexier to live the life that Sayers lived than the life that Brian did.

I will never know what helped Brian remain so deeply engaged or what motivated his choices. I will never know what he was feeling during the years depicted in this film. What I do know is how deeply his story resonates for me, albeit in different ways, over the course of my life. Watching the movie *Brian's Song* was like a Rorshach test for me. Same set of images, yet wildly different interpretations. It is a story that lives within me and has helped me identify and recognize what I value most: relationships, grit, and persistence. I want to remain deeply engaged and ready to play. I want to be there for the people in my life. I want to give both my work, and those with whom I work and live, my all.

∝

What is the value, the rightness, or the
truth of the work you feel called to do?
Who are the specific people you struggle for?

Practice

Today, reflect upon the relationships in your life that matter most to you. Throughout the day, make a point to thank all those who bring joy to your life.

Acknowledgments

The best part about writing a book about deepening engagement is the opportunity it gave me to engage deeply in conversation with so many wise colleagues and friends. Thank you Elizabeth Jarrett Andrew, Melissa Borgmann-Kiemde, Tawanna Brown, Sandhya Purohit Caton, JoEllen Windau Cattapan, Mary Cavanaugh, Tom Darnall, Dianne DelGiorno, Kim DeLong and the Family Matters community, Mohamed Dukuly, Jennifer Grant Haworth, Paul Hayes, François Kiemde, Michelle L'Allier, Amy Zalk Larson, LeeAnn McCarthy, Christine Luna Munger, Bonnie Sherman, Bob Stains, Marty Stortz, and Lew Zeidner for your willingness to offer feedback on one or more of the chapters in this book, along with your permission to feature your stories.

As I embarked upon the path of identifying evocative quotations and poems to highlight the theme of each chapter, I became the grateful beneficiary of four original poems written specifically for this book by poets Jennifer (Jinks) Hoffmann and Jeannie Roberts. Thank you, Jinks and Jeannie, for the gift of your work and your friendship as well as all the time you so generously shared offering responses to many of the chapters.

After I began writing the book, some marvelous unexpected sources of wisdom emerged. In particular, I am grateful to Rob Lehman at the Fetzer Insitute for his affirmative and gracious response to my request to talk about his understanding of deep engagement. Rob, along with Bob Boisture, Deborah Yeager, and Kathy Cavanaugh of the Fetzer Institute, kindly offered their time, observations, questions, and internal documents related to the Institute's practice of deep engagement as a model of community and board governance.

Other sources of wisdom and encouragement that sustain me are my colleagues Kathleen Cahalan, Laura Kelly Fanucci, and Ryan Corcoran, with whom I have the privilege of working on the *Lives Explored* video narrative series (for the Collegeville Institute Seminars on Vocation, funded by the Lilly Endowment, Inc.). Some of my most memorable lessons about building communities of engagement were indelibly shaped through my work as a consultant for the Religion Division at the Lilly Endowment, Inc. I am especially grateful to Chris Coble, Craig Dykstra, Kim Maphis Early, Elizabeth Lynn, Susie Quern Pratt, Susan Weber, and John Wimmer.

From the get-go, my beloved editor Emily Wichland at SkyLight Paths let me know she was a champion of this project. Emily, along with all those with whom she works at SkyLight Paths, consistently models for me the art of collaboration and respectful, mutual engagement in giving birth to a book. It is an honor to work with all of you.

So much of my work focuses on inviting others to reflect and identify where they are finding purpose, meaning, and joy in their lives. For me, my immense joy begins and ends at home. I am particularly blessed to share my life with my husband, Mark, and our son, Ryan. Mark is a continuous source of inspiration for me. He has a far more expansive menu than mine (and actually does use nothing but the freshest ingredients), and I am grateful for the many ways he has nourished my life over the past thirty years. Together we rejoice and continue to learn from our young adult son, Ryan, as we watch him create his path for leading a life of deep engagement.

Last, but by no means least, I have been blessed to have two parents who each, in their own way, lead lives of deep engagement. I dedicate this book to them in gratitude for their examples and for their unfailing trust that I would find my own distinctive way to do the same.

Notes

Introduction

1. *Lives Explored* is a production of the Collegeville Institute Seminars on Vocation and is funded through the generosity of the Lilly Endowment, Inc. Visit www.lives-explored.com to view François's story and the entire collection of narratives featured in this series.
2. www.lives-explored.com.
3. Bob Johansen, *Leaders Make the Future: Ten New Leadership Skills for an Uncertain World* (San Francisco: Berrett-Koehler Publishers, 2012), 1.
4. Howard Thurman, "The Sound of the Genuine," Baccalaureate Address at Spelman College, May 4, 1980, edited by Jo Moore Stewart for *The Spelman Messenger* 96 no. 4 (Summer 1980): 14–15.
5. Ibid.
6. Ibid.
7. Ibid.

Part One: Engaging Our True Self

1. Stephen Cope, *The Great Work of Your Life: A Guide for the Journey to Your True Calling* (New York: Bantam Books, 2012), 42.
2. Ibid., 44.
3. Ibid., 42.
4. Wayne Muller, *Sabbath: Finding Rest, Renewal, and Delight in Our Busy Lives* (New York: Bantam Books, 2000), 85.
5. Elizabeth Yates, *Howard Thurman—Portrait of a Practical Dreamer* (New York: The John Day Company, 1964), 26.
6. Thurman, "The Sound of the Genuine," 14–15.

7. Lawrence Ferlinghetti, *How to Paint Sunlight: Lyric Poems & Others (1997–2000)* (New York: New Directions, 2002), 57–58.

8. Jacques Lusseyran, *And There Was Light: The Extraordinary Memoir of a Blind Hero of the French Resistance in World War II*, 4th. ed. (Novato, CA: New World Library, 2014), 11–14.

9. Ibid., 15.

10. David Ulrich, *The Widening Stream: The Seven Stages of Creativity* (Hillsboro, OR: Beyond Words Publishing, 2002), xxv.

11. Martha Beck, *Finding Your Own North Star: Claiming the Life You Were Meant to Live* (New York: Three Rivers Press, 2001), 45, 54.

12. One of the dominant frameworks for understanding grief has been, and continues to be, that of Elisabeth Kübler-Ross. Kübler-Ross identified an understanding of the stages of grief based on her experience of listening to and observing people with terminal diagnoses. Later in life, she conveyed that her conceptualization of the emotions that accompanied dying was never intended as a way to strategize grief. She clarified that, rather than put forth a stage theory—denial, anger, bargaining, depression, acceptance—her intent was to identify the features of the terrain. There is no template for grieving. Just as two persons who share the same experience may construct very different narratives about their experience, no two people experience the same loss (for example, the loss of a loved one) in the same way.

13. www.angelesarrien.com.

Part Two: Engaging One Another

1. Evelyn Underhill, *Practical Mysticism* (Alpharetta, GA: First Ariel Press, 1986), 29.

2. Robert Fritz, *The Path of Least Resistance: Learning to Become the Creative Force in Your Own Life*, rev. ed. (New York: Fawcett Columbine, 1989), 231.

3. Jack Kornfield, *The Wise Heart: A Guide to the Universal Teachings of Buddhist Psychology* (New York: Bantam Books, 2008), 371–72.

4. I am grateful to Amy Zalk Larson for offering me another interpretation of this story.

5. www.lindastone.net.

6. Kevin Cashman, *The Pause Principle: Step Back to Lead Forward* (San Francisco: Berrett-Koehler Publishers, 2012), 15.

7. Ibid., 21.

8. You will find all the Touchstones for participating in Circles of Trust at www.couragerenewal.org/touchstones.

9. Bob Kelly, *Worth Repeating: More Than 5,000 Classic and Contemporary Quotes* (Grand Rapids, MI: Kregel Publications, 2003), 263.

10. Jalal al-Din Rumi, "Two Kinds of Intelligence," in *The Essential Rumi,* trans. Coleman Barks with John Moyne, A. J. Arberry, and Reynold Nicholson (New York: HarperOne, 2004), 178.

11. David Whyte, *Crossing the Unknown Sea: Work as a Pilgrimage of Identity* (New York: Riverhead Books, 2001), 238.

12. Douglas Steere, *Gleanings: A Random Harvest* (Nashville: Upper Room, 1986), 83.

13. Dave Isay, *Ties That Bind: Stories of Love and Gratitude from the First Ten Years of StoryCorps* (New York: Penguin Press, 2013), 2–3.

14. Edgar Schein, *Humble Inquiry: The Gentle Art of Asking Instead of Telling* (San Francisco: Berrett-Koehler Publishers, 2013), 9.

15. Ibid., 21.

16. Carole Dweck, *Mindset: The New Psychology of Success* (New York: Ballantine Books, 2006), 235.

17. Ellen Langer, *Counter-Clockwise: Mindful Health and the Power of Possibility* (New York: Ballantine Books, 2009), 18–19.

Part Three: Cultivating Engaging Communities

1. Ann Patchett, *What Now?* (New York: HarperCollins, 2008), 22.

2. *Fetzer Institute's Shared Agreements for a Community of Freedom: A Handbook of Values, Practices, and Policies* (Kalamazoo, MI: Fetzer Institute, 1998), 91. Rob recalls his impressions as a participant in those initial conversations: "He was talking about some sort of spiritual vessel.... As I look back today, I see those early conversations with John pointing to two organizational ideas of great importance to him: that the institute is a mission-centered organization focused for the long term on love, and the institute is community-centered and rooted in freedom.... One cannot exist without the other. There can be no outer expression of love without inner freedom, and no true inner freedom without an outer expression of love."

3. The group that plans these weekly gatherings consists of a cross-section of representatives from each area of the organization. The top ten topics for these Community of Freedom gatherings was determined by a staff survey: communicating effectively; emotional intelligence; values work; building, grounds, and logo symbolism; teambuilding; leadership; community; mindfulness; vocation; and brightening our true colors (that is, personality and work style assessment).

4. Peter Block, *The Answer to How Is Yes: Acting on What Matters* (San Francisco: Berrett-Koehler Publishers, 2002), 1.

5. Gervase Bushe, "Five Theories of Change Embedded in Appreciative Inquiry," in *Appreciative Inquiry: Foundations in Positive Organization Development*, eds. David Cooperrider, Peter Sorenson, Therese Yeager, and Diana Whitney (Champaign, IL: Stipes, 2005), 121–32.

6. Susan Stabile, *Growing in Love and Wisdom: Tibetan Buddhist Sources for Christian Meditation* (New York: Oxford University Press, 2013), 106. For further information on the practice of *tonglen*, see Pema Chödrön's books, especially *Start Where You Are: A Guide to Compassionate Living* (Boston: Shambhala Publications, 2001).

7. http://topmoralstories.blogspot.com/2008/05/bad-news-good-news-who-knows.html.

8. Pema Chödrön, *When Things Fall Apart: Heart Advice for Difficult Times* (Boston: Shambhala Publications, 1997), 8–9.

9. John Paul Lederach, *The Moral Imagination: The Art and Soul of Building Peace* (New York: Oxford University Press, 2005), 71.

10. Ibid., 72.

11. "PBS NewsHour," www.pbs.org/newshour/bb/entertainment/july-dec10/herbie_09-16.html (accessed October 2, 2012).

12. See Eknath Easwaran's translation, *The Bhagavad Gita* (Tomales, CA: Nilgiri Press, 1985), 66. From the Gita, chapter 2, verse 47: "You have the right to work, but never to the fruit of work. You should never engage in action for the sake of reward, nor should you long for inaction." In Hindu philosophy, spiritual perfection is not attained by abandoning action, but by giving a new meaning to action—that of detaching from the outcome of our actions, that is, being impartial to failure and success.

For Further Reading

Beck, Martha. *Finding Your Own North Star: Claiming the Life You Were Meant to Live.* New York: Three Rivers Press, 2001.

Benefiel, Margaret. *Soul at Work: Spiritual Leadership in Organizations.* New York: Seabury Books, 2005.

Block, Peter. *The Answer to How Is Yes: Acting on What Matters.* San Francisco: Berrett-Koehler Publishers, 2002.

Brown, Judy. *The Art and Spirit of Leadership.* Bloomington, IN: Trafford Publishing, 2012.

———. *A Leader's Guide to Reflective Practice.* Bloomington, IN: Trafford Publishing, 2007.

Bushe, Gervase. "Five Theories of Change Embedded in Appreciative Inquiry." In *Appreciative Inquiry: Foundations in Positive Organization Development.* Edited by David Cooperrider, Peter Sorenson, Therese Yeager, and Diana Whitney. Champaign, IL: Stipes Publishing, 2005.

Cannon, Moya. *The Parchment Boat.* New York: Gallery Books, 1998.

Cashman, Kevin. *Leadership from the Inside Out: Becoming a Leader for Life.* San Francisco: Berrett-Koehler Publishers, 2008.

———. *The Pause Principle: Step Back to Lead Forward.* San Francisco: Berrett-Koehler Publishers, 2012.

Chödrön, Pema. *When Things Fall Apart: Heart Advice for Difficult Times.* Boston: Shambhala Publications, 1997.

———. *The Wisdom of No Escape.* Boston: Shambhala Publications, 2001.

Cope, Stephen. *The Great Work of Your Life: A Guide for the Journey to Your True Calling.* New York: Bantam Books, 2012.

De Mille, Agnes. *Martha: The Life and Work of Martha Graham—A Biography.* New York: Random House, 1991.

Dweck, Carol. *Mindset: The New Psychology of Success.* New York: Ballantine Books, 2006.

Emerson, Ralph Waldo. *The Spiritual Emerson: Essential Works by Ralph Waldo Emerson.* New York: Jeremy P. Tarcher/Penguin, 2008.

Ferlinghetti, Lawrence. "Into the Interior." In *How to Paint Sunlight: Lyric Poems & Others (1997–2000).* New York: New Directions, 2002.

Fritz, Robert. *The Path of Least Resistance: Learning to Become the Creative Force in Your Own Life,* rev. ed. New York: Fawcett Columbine, 1989.

Hammarskjöld, Dag. *Markings.* New York: Alfred A. Knopf, 1972.

Hart, Tobin. *The Four Virtues: Presence, Heart, Wisdom, Creation.* New York: Simon and Schuster, 2014.

Heath, Chip, and Dan Heath. *Switch: How to Change Things When Change Is Hard.* New York: Broadway Books, 2010.

Helminski, Kabir. *Living Presence: A Sufi Way to Mindfulness and the Essential Self.* New York: Penguin Putnam, 1992.

Isay, Dave, ed. *Ties That Bind: Stories of Love and Gratitude from the First Ten Years of StoryCorps.* New York: Penguin Press, 2013.

Johansen, Bob. *Leaders Make the Future: Ten New Leadership Skills for an Uncertain World.* San Francisco: Berrett-Koehler Publishers, 2012.

Johnstone, Keith. *Impro: Improvisation and the Theatre.* New York: Routledge, 1981.

Kornfield, Jack. *The Wise Heart: A Guide to the Universal Teachings of Buddhist Psychology.* New York: Bantam Books, 2008.

Langer, Ellen. *Counter-Clockwise: Mindful Health and the Power of Possibility.* New York: Ballantine Books, 2009.

Lao-Tzu. *Tao Te Ching.* Translated by Stephen Mitchell. New York: Harper & Row, 1988.

Lederach, John Paul. *The Moral Imagination: The Art and Soul of Building Peace.* New York: Oxford University Press, 2005.

Levoy, Gregg. *Callings: Finding and Following an Authentic Life.* New York: Three Rivers Press, 1997.

Lindbergh, Anne Morrow. *Gift from the Sea.* New York: Random House, 1955.

Loehr, Jim, and Tony Schwartz. *The Power of Full Engagement: Managing Energy, Not Time, Is the Key to High Performance and Personal Renewal.* New York: Free Press, 2003.

Lusseyran, Jacques. *And There Was Light: The Extraordinary Memoir of a Blind Hero of the French Resistance in World War II,* 4th. ed. Novato, CA: New World Library, 2014.

Lyubomirsky, Sonja. *The Myths of Happiness: What Should Make You Happy But Doesn't, What Shouldn't Make You Happy But Does.* New York: Penguin Press, 2013.

Machado, Antonio. "Last Night, As I was Sleeping." In *Times Alone: Selected Poems of Antonio Machado.* Translated by Robert Bly. Middletown, CT: Wesleyan University Press, 1983.

Merton, Thomas. *The Hidden Ground of Love: Letters by Thomas Merton on Religious Experience and Social Concerns.* Edited by William Shannon. New York: Farrar, Strauss and Giroux, 1993.

Millis, Diane M. *Conversation—The Sacred Art: Practicing Presence in an Age of Distraction.* Woodstock, VT: SkyLight Paths Publishing, 2013.

Muller, Wayne. *Sabbath: Finding Rest, Renewal, and Delight in Our Busy Lives.* New York: Bantam Books, 2000.

O'Donohue, John. *Anam Cara: Spiritual Wisdom from the Celtic World.* London: Bantam Books, 1997.

Palmer, Parker J. *A Hidden Wholeness: The Journey toward an Undivided Life.* San Francisco: Jossey-Bass, 2004.

————. *Let Your Life Speak: Listening for the Voice of Vocation.* San Francisco: Jossey-Bass, 2000.

Patchett, Ann. *What Now?* New York: HarperCollins, 2008.

Remen, Rachel Naomi. *My Grandfather's Blessings: Stories of Strength, Refuge, and Belonging.* New York: Riverhead Books, 2000.

Rumi, Jalal al-Din. *The Essential Rumi.* Translated by Coleman Barks with John Moyne, A. J. Arberry, and Reynold Nicholson. New York: HarperOne, 2004.

Schein, Edgar. *Humble Inquiry: The Gentle Art of Asking Instead of Telling.* San Francisco: Berrett-Koehler Publishers, 2013.

Stabile, Susan. *Growing in Love and Wisdom: Tibetan Buddhist Sources for Christian Meditation.* New York: Oxford University Press, 2013.

Steere, Douglas. *Gleanings: A Random Harvest.* Nashville: Upper Room, 1986.

————. *On Being Present Where You Are.* Wallingford, PA: Pendle Hill Publications, 1967.

Thurman, Howard. "The Sound of the Genuine." Baccalaureate Address at Spelman College, May 4, 1980. Edited by Jo Moore Stewart for *The Spelman Messenger* 96, no. 4 (Summer 1980): 14–15.

Ulrich, David. *The Widening Stream: The Seven Stages of Creativity.* Hillsboro, OR: Beyond Words Publishing, 2002.

Wheatley, Margaret. *So Far from Home: Lost and Found in Our Brave New World.* San Francisco: Berrett-Koehler Publishers, 2012.

————. *Turning to One Another: Simple Conversations to Restore Hope to the Future*, 2nd ed. San Francisco: Berrett-Koehler Publishers, 2009.

Whyte, David. *Crossing the Unknown Sea: Work as a Pilgrimage of Identity.* New York: Riverhead Books, 2001.

————. "The Winter of Listening." In *The House of Belonging*. Langley, WA: Many Rivers Press, 1997.

Yates, Elizabeth. *Howard Thurman—Portrait of a Practical Dreamer.* New York: The John Day Company, 1964.

Zander, Benjamin, and Rosamund Stone Zander. *The Art of Possibility: Transforming Professional and Personal Life.* Boston: Harvard Business School Press, 2000.

Credits

About SKYLIGHT PATHS Publishing

SkyLight Paths Publishing is creating a place where people of different spiritual traditions come together for challenge and inspiration, a place where we can help each other understand the mystery that lies at the heart of our existence.

Through spirituality, our religious beliefs are increasingly becoming a part of our lives—rather than *apart* from our lives. While many of us may be more interested than ever in spiritual growth, we may be less firmly planted in traditional religion. Yet, we do want to deepen our relationship to the sacred, to learn from our own as well as from other faith traditions, and to practice in new ways.

SkyLight Paths sees both believers and seekers as a community that increasingly transcends traditional boundaries of religion and denomination—people wanting to learn from each other, *walking together, finding the way*.

For your information and convenience, at the back of this book we have provided a list of other SkyLight Paths books you might find interesting and useful. They cover the following subjects:

Buddhism / Zen	Gnosticism	Poetry
Catholicism	Hinduism / Vedanta	Prayer
Chaplaincy		Religious Etiquette
Children's Books	Inspiration	Retirement & Later-Life Spirituality
Christianity	Islam / Sufism	
Comparative Religion	Judaism	Spiritual Biography
	Meditation	Spiritual Direction
Earth-Based Spirituality	Mindfulness	Spirituality
	Monasticism	Women's Interest
Enneagram	Mysticism	Worship
Global Spiritual Perspectives	Personal Growth	